A PEDIATRIC PLAY PROGRAM

A PEDIATRIC PLAY PROGRAM

DEVELOPING A THERAPEUTIC PLAY PROGRAM
FOR CHILDREN IN MEDICAL SETTINGS

By

PAT AZARNOFF, B.S., M.Ed.
Coordinator, Pediatric Clinic Play Program
Department of Pediatrics
University of California, Los Angeles

and

SHARON FLEGAL, B.A.
Formerly Child Activity Director
Pediatric Inpatient Unit
University of California, Los Angeles

With a Foreword By

T. BERRY BRAZELTON, M.D.
Department of Pediatrics
Harvard Medical School
Boston, Massachusetts

CHARLES C THOMAS • PUBLISHER
Springfield • Illinois • U.S.A.

Published and Distributed Throughout the World by
CHARLES C THOMAS • PUBLISHER
Bannerstone House
301-327 East Lawrence Avenue, Springfield, Illinois, U.S.A.

ISBN 0-398-03272-6
Library of Congress Catalog Card Number: 74 12061

With THOMAS BOOKS careful attention is given to all details of manufacturing and design. It is the Publisher's desire to present books that are satisfactory as to their physical qualities and artistic possibilities and appropriate for their particular use. THOMAS BOOKS will be true to those laws of quality that assure a good name and good will.

Printed in the United States of America
I-1

Library of Congress Cataloging in Publication Data

Azarnoff, Pat.
A pediatric play program.

Bibliography: p.
1. Children—Hospital care. 2. Play therapy.
I. Flegal, Sharon, joint author. II. Title.
[DNLM: 1. Hospital administration. 2. Play therapy.
WM450 A992p]
RJ242.A9 362.7'8'11 74-12061
ISBN 0-398-03272-6

FOREWORD

THIS CONCISE BOOK tells how to set up a therapeutic play program for children in hospitals and clinics. It is literally chock full of homely wisdom for those who need the push or the encouragement to start an activities program for sick children and their parents. The authors are very sensitive to the pressures on the staff of a busy hospital and even an ill-equipped hospital. They speak with sensitivity to many hospitals or institutions who use "inadequate funds" as an argument for not responding to the psychological needs of the children in their care.

As I read the simple instructions in this lovely book, it became obvious that it is not the equipment alone that matters, but the atmosphere of caring on the part of the staff and the formal attempts to demonstrate this caring by shaping one's efforts to what each child needs. The authors have obviously worked long and hard for their wisdom. They are convincing in their plea for an active approach to helping children recover who are ill and separated from their family surroundings. They believe, as I do, that an illness and a hospitalization *can* be a positive learning experience for children.

The attitude of looking for the strengths in a child's reactions and interactions and reinforcing them comes through powerfully in the book you are about to read. It adds practical suggestions and convincing advice about how to treat the child with respect for his capacity to cope and a caring for his individual needs to make it more possible for his medical experience to become an opportunity for learning about himself!

Parents also can be helped to regard hospitalization as a learning encounter. By finding new ways of helping their child, realizing that their own efforts to aid the child's recovery are important in furthering his mastery of a potentially traumatic experience, hospitalization may become a positive factor for them and a move toward improvement of the parent-child relationship.

This book was written on the premise that such a large order could be accomplished. Physicians are increasingly aware that treating a child's illness and helping him with physical recovery is not enough. Crises offer us a chance to promote the child's development and help him build a better life. Because this book emphasizes the need and value of concentrating on the child in this way instead of only on the treatment of his disease it will help to promote better care for children in medical settings.

T. Berry Brazelton, M.D.

INTRODUCTION

When doctors, nurses or administrators of a pediatric unit in the hospital or clinic decide they want to significantly improve the emotional environment of their young patients by introducing a play program, certain initial questions will occur to them. How can they begin? Who should be hired? In what way can a playroom be organized? Which toys, supplies and materials are needed? How can volunteers assist in the program? These questions and others equally important are answered in this book. Problems related to typical low budgets and minimal staffing are also given attention.

Play directors, pediatric nurses, parents or volunteers who already have the use of a playroom may be seeking activitics that are suitable to the restrictions of a medical setting and therapeutic for the children who are involved. Specific suggestions are provided here as well as ways of adapting these activities to each child.

No program can be developed without support. Yet sometimes the most vocal supporters unwittingly throw barriers in the way of developing a program. You will find some of the most frequently heard objections to a mentally healthy atmosphere for children presented here and discussed.

Children in the medical milieu not only have the same developmental requirements which they had before they entered the hospital or clinic but they also have new needs, having to adjust and adapt to difficulties never before encountered. With the necessary materials, space to play and with specially trained people, children can be helped to cope successfully with these difficulties and to master them, coming out of the experience stronger than before.

There has been considerable writing elsewhere of the enormous impact on children of both positive and negative medical experiences. We have provided a selected bibliography which offers other ideas and suggestions to the professional, as well as a listing of children's books.

In addition to our work with children in several hospitals and clinics we have discussed with many professional colleagues from various child-oriented fields what obstacles they have faced and what has worked for them. Therefore, while this book is based on theoretical considerations, it offers practical ideas tested by the authors.

This work was supported in part by NIII rcsearch grant #MH-22856 from the Mental Health Service Development Branch, (Arthur H. Parmelee, M.D., principal investigator). We also gratefully acknowledge the support of the Frederick R. Weisman family and the UCLA Medical Center Auxiliary.

In this writing and in our work, people interested in the benefits children derive from play and from therapeutic relationships, were continuously and greatly encouraging. Particularly helpful were Arthur H. Parmelee, M.D., T. Berry Brazelton, M.D., Walter Tasem, M.D., Charlotte Neumann, M.D., Richard Casady, M.D., David Fleisher, M.D., Roberta Deutschman, Mary Ferrero, Beth Treadway, R.N., Ruth Wester, R.N., Herlinda Lozano, Eleanor Wasson, Maurice Baum, Ph.D., Estelle Parness, Rose Bromwich, Tracy Susman and those special people—Carl, Ryan, Roy, Julie and Karen.

P. A.
S. F.

CONTENTS

A PEDIATRIC PLAY PROGRAM

Chapter 1

DESCRIBING A PLAY PROGRAM

Play is basic to the ways in which children learn about themselves and the world around them. Through directed play activities, the child can better understand the experiences of the hospital and communicate his fears and misunderstandings of the various aspects of his illness and required treatment. In this chapter, the various functions of an inhospital therapeutic play program will be discussed.

The most important function of a pediatric play program is to assist the medical staff in providing better health care. The evidence clearly shows that psychological stress and the trauma of hospitalization can in some cases impede physical recovery. Less well-documented, but frequently observed, is that a properly run therapeutic play program can help children recover faster. A play program which considers the psychological as well as the physical problems of the child will lessen the impact of hospitalization and the resulting psychological damage and disruption to the child's developing personality.

For many children hospitalization becomes *a positive growth experience* as they expand their capacities to cope with a new environment, with unaccustomed separations from their parents, with immobilization during a treatment, with fear, with pain, or with something as "simple" as different foods and faces. In general a play program which considers the psychological as well as the physical problems of the child will lessen the impact of hospitalization on recovery and can result in shorter hospital stays.

The most obvious manner in which the play program can help in health care is when physical activity needs to be encouraged or discouraged. Physical restraints are less necessary to immobilize a child when he is involved in play. A child is not going to think of pulling out a tube or scratching a patched eye if he is enjoying meaningful activity. Fewer nets are seen covering cribs of active children when they are allowed to expend some of their energy through play.

> A fourteen-year-old boy with osteomyelitis of the spine challenged the doctor's orders and pretended to himself, and to personnel, that he was not on bedrest. He ignored the doctor's warnings about the possibility of permanent spinal damage at this point in his illness. However, when he and the play director designed a basketball hoop to hang over his bed and he had daily, therapeutic, directed activity, the boy was able to relax and to more calmly tolerate his medical restrictions.

Play activity may also be designed to encourage needed movement for the child who has undergone surgery. Movement can help to clear up or to prevent lung congestion. The child who has participated in a play program before surgery finds participation and ambulation are easier after surgery because he has something to look forward to and the activities are familiar.

The examination or treatment of a fearful child can often be done more quickly and with less physical restraint when a child has been properly prepared through the play program. Many of the experiences provided by such a program are designed to encourage an active role in treatment rather than passivity by the child. As a result, when the child is called upon to do something during medical treatment, he has the benefit of having been educated and encouraged during play, so he can do what is required rather than just have procedures done to him. Less stress is thereby caused to both patient and staff.

Another important aspect of the play program is to *provide the medical staff with a more normal setting in which to observe their patients.* Doctors often remark how different their young patients look when involved in meaningful play as compared to how they appear when lying in bed. Observations of this kind aid the physicians in deciding changes in treatment, prescription of pain medication or even an order to be discharged. Thus the play program helps sort out complaints of pain from attention-getting behavior.

Laurie, a nine-year-old, came into the hospital after a five month history of stomach aches. Bent at the waist, she walked holding her stomach and the side rail. Her admitting doctor gave no orders for immediate tests, allowing Laurie some time to become as comfortable as possible in the hospital.

The play specialist found that Laurie, distracted into a game of catch, would let go of her stomach, walk quickly and even stoop to pick up a dropped ball. Occasionally, she seemed to remember her pain and would clutch her abdomen. During a game of cards between the play director, Laurie and Laurie's visiting girlfriends, Laurie became involved to the point of laughing. Whenever her mother came into the room, however, Laurie whined and complained of pain.

Behavioral observations such as these are invaluable to the physician. Because hospital beds and examining rooms are not the best place for assessment of these problems, observations by playroom staff in both settings can provide doctors with this assessment *as the child engages in normal play.* A play specialist helps identify unusual behavior or physical performance as well, and can observe in various situations: with and without parents; with and without siblings or peers; in active or quiet play; in self-directed or adult-directed play; using small manipulative objects or toys needing large muscles; under stress or in a low-demand, relaxed atmosphere. The play director has a chance to make observations testing previous observations. Thus another dimension is added to the examination process. Results can be briefly and comprehensively added to the medical records and recommendations made accordingly.

Many physicians report the increase of patients who have behavioral or school problems and psychosomatic complaints. Parents are becoming more interested in seeking medical advice for problems they would not have expected the doctor to help with years ago: disturbances of sleep, deviations of speech, prevention of accident, traveling with children, estimates of readiness for nursery school, poor peer relationships and problems in school. The play specialist can provide knowledgeable advice in these areas.

Another aim of a play program conducted by trained personnel is to promote learning and relieve anxieties connected with the medical setting. Play is generally neglected as an important aid to the ill or disabled youngster who uses it to understand what is happening to him. But through observing the child's play the play director often perceives anxiety-producing situations which nurses or doctors may miss. These might include concerns over problems in the family, siblings who are as confused as the patient, overprotective parents or misconceptions about the medical treatment. The play director can help staff and parents understand what reactions children have had to their hospital or clinic experience. This kind of feedback is needed for helping adults to reassure children to clear up frightening misconceptions the children might have.

> Before his test, six-year-old Jim played with the simulated, miniaturized heart catheterization machine. Most of his play centered on giving shots and repeating tests. When the play director asked why the doll had to have so many, he said, "because the baby did something wrong." She then asked why he, Jim, had to have the test and he replied that it was because he was bad, too!
>
> With further play and comments, the director elicited from Jim the reason he thought he might be in the hospital. This time the answer was "because my blood doesn't go through right." The director assured him that this was a reasonable answer. The parents were then encouraged to further explain the real medical reasons for his stay in the hospital, to reassure him that he was a good boy, that they loved him and that he would soon go home to stay.

A child is encouraged to cooperate with adult expectations under a wide variety of situations. He may be told to pick up his toys, say thank you to the neighbor who gave him a cookie or talk so everyone in class can hear. The expected behavior for these demands is learned gradually and through situations in which the child usually understands the reasons for the demands. However, many of the demands imposed on the hospitalized child are sudden and foreign to him and seem to make little sense. Appropriate play helps the child release these tensions, express frustrations and confront reality. The interpretation of this play to adults who wish to help the child is useful.

An organized play program can help a child post-operatively to overcome his initial fear of ridicule and rejection. It can ease his fears about his changed body and increase his social adjustment, through interaction with other children.

Eight-year-old John had undergone urologic surgery and the doctors asked the play director to encourage walking. But John hesitated about walking to the play area and joining into the activities. The director brought several children to his room. They talked about the times he used to come to the playroom and the fun they had. "Yes," John replied, "but that was before I had *this*," and he pointed to the urine-collecting bag attached to the bed. "Oh," shrugged one of the other children, "I used to have one of those and I didn't like it either."

The director asked the child if he had ever gone to the playroom with it and he said he had. She asked if people seemed to pay attention to it and he said they did not. Encouraged though cautious, John went into the playroom eventually, thereby satisfying the doctor's requirements for physical activity. Perhaps equally important he was able to overcome a psychological hurdle.

A patient and his family need to have this kind of information, reassurance and consistent attention. The child needs to know that the people who are caring for him understand his fears and will answer his questions in a sympathetic and knowledgeable way. Someone should be available to talk with the child and family supportively in this way and respond to their psychological needs. This notion of caring about the reactions of a child and his family to a potentially traumatic situation is an integral part of the philosophy of a therapeutic play program.

A pediatric play program also seeks to maintain normal development and provide support to families before, during and after hospitalization. Some hospitals provide preadmission tours of the pediatric unit or a storybook about coming to the hospital. Others send a staff person or health science student on a home visit prior to hospitalization.

In the outpatient clinic the play director takes many opportunities to work with children individually. This one-to-one ratio is invaluable in an atmosphere which often must sacrifice quiet consideration to efficiency and where loneliness and apprehension are endemic. Often, when someone is hospitalized, his physical limitation or illness may be focused on to the exclusion of his more healthy physical parts or his feelings. Some illnesses become so overwhelming to the patient that he is unable to focus on anything else. This may be especially true for the patient with a life-threatening disease. Attending a clinic regularly or being hospitalized is a frequent reminder to the patient that he is ill and his painful feelings of grief, anger, guilt, helplessness, fear or despair may be activated. These emotional reactions to illness, which inhibit desirable growth can be dealt with through play and structured verbal exchanges such as:

—Play groups
—Scheduled parent discussion groups
—Informal parent discussion groups
—Child discussion groups
—Meetings arranged between the parents and staff doctors

In addition the clinic playroom staff can coordinate observations of children's reactions to medical care with the staff on the inpatient unit. They can begin the preparation of those children who will require hospitalization. Children with chronic conditions who will have repeated hospitalizations can maintain continuity with the total staff on the unit with occasional visits to them when they come for outpatient care. Returning to the hospital then is not as traumatizing as it might otherwise be for a child.

An outpatient playroom provides a safe place for a patient's siblings to wait, which is comforting to worried or harassed parents of a sick child. This means that doctors as well as technicians in the laboratory areas can attend the young patient and talk with his parents without the noise and interference of other children. Siblings need to know what is happening, however, and if it will happen to them. The play program provides an excellent opportunity through which to explore these questions and feelings. The play director can provide reassurance to the siblings and informally assess their understanding in order to provide them with adequate information and reassurance, with the parents' permission. When necessary, this may be bolstered by bringing the sibling to see the areas in the hospital or clinic he has heard about—for instance, to see the radiology rooms or the lab where sister gets her blood tested every week.

A play program staff member should *not* be regarded as a baby-sitter. He or she can offer an informal program of health education, positive attitudes about self-care and about health personnel and procedures, and in the outpatient clinic opportunities for the children of adult patients to reach out for help in coping with the crisis of illness.

In the hospital a young child *needs* a parent as often as possible, but few hospitals have been designed to include parent participation in medical care. *The introduction of a play director as liaison may assist parents in their involvement.* Although parents can give love and attention to their child as no one else can, some parents do not ordinarily play with their youngsters at home; so, when the child is hospitalized and the parents and child are under stress, organized, continuous play is difficult for these parents to sustain. They can be helped to learn about their children by being able to observe them in a play group or in a playroom that offers several interest centers guided by trained personnel. The parent may enter into play or talk with his child if he wishes, but he will not feel compelled to entertain, amuse or divert this child beyond the limits of his own experience, habit or temperament.

Playroom activities and personnel give parents an opportunity to engage in informal discussion about childrearing or, if any parents prefer, to arrange a conference for more specific consideration of their children.

The play program that has served parents as well as children will be most effective in preventive work for post-hospital family problems. By observing the interactions between parents and child and the way the child has coped with his hospitalization, the play director can provide suggestions regarding future probable behavior once the child goes home. It may help the mother to know ahead of time that it is not unusual for her two-year-old to feel less secure at home than he was before hospitalization.

Sally cried and clung to her mother every time visiting hours were over. The play director talked with Sally's mother about gradual separations during which she tells Sally she will be right back, goes into the next room for just a minute and then returns, reemphasizing the fact that she came back as she said she would. The play director suggested that these short separations be increased in time until Sally can again tolerate being left alone. Soon after discharge Sally was able to stay with a babysitter for an evening without an adverse reaction.

Upon discharge, doctors tell patients and their parents what to expect and what to be careful of in regard to physical problems. If the patient needs a convalescent period, the doctor recommends when the child can begin normal activity. The physician, however, seldom recommends substitute activities to help the child through convalescence or talks with the parents about possible behavior changes. An overworked physician may ask for help in both instances from the therapeutic play director. She can be informative about the variety of suitable activities during convalescence and can adjust her recommendations to such factors as the amount of time the mother has available for the child, the length of convalescence, any particular body parts which might need more or less activity and the child's ability to play quietly by himself or with other children.

Especially in need of helpful suggestions is the family of the child being discharged with severe physical limitations. For instance, the child who must wear a body cast for a number of months will undoubtedly have more trouble adjusting to it if he is bored than if he has satisfying activities in which to engage.

Every place in the medical building that serves children should offer an atmosphere and programs responsive to the children's needs. For children view many medical procedures as confusing and threatening no matter where they take place: in a doctor's office, hospital or outpatient clinic. Although hospitalization adds the additional anxiety of separation from the family, the clinic may be frightening, too. The clinic remains a place in which children can perceive examinations and treatment procedures as invasive, threatening and restrictive. Therefore, they need reassurance, information and autonomy in clinics as well as in hospitals, and both places need trained behavioral specialists to assist in pediatric work.

A medical facility should provide more than just medical treatment. It should look to the well-being of the whole person, whether a patient or a parent or a child of a patient. Besides considering minimizing disturbing environmental factors such as no play area, lengthy waiting periods, indifference to safety, poor lighting, lack of seating, scarcity of drinking fountains, height of phones and long distances to restrooms, consideration should also be given to the staff who contact the patient and his family.

Staff members who are unresponsive to patients' needs invite hostility, restlessness and anger. How many broken clinic appointments are attributable to the atmosphere and abuse which patients sometimes have to endure? It is simply good business to be kind. How much of the disruptive and demanding behavior of hospitalized children is the result of frustrated natural needs for a safe and comfortable play environment in which to express the feelings and expend the energies that result from their state of tension and ill health?

Chapter 2

HOUSING A PLAY PROGRAM

There are several areas in which the patients' emotional and social needs can be served. Though the staff and materials vary, the environment alone can be an important factor in relieving anxiety. Coordination of services among these various departments amplifies the benefits children will receive.

Inpatient Play Areas

THE INPATIENT UNIT is the medical setting best known for its use of a therapeutic play program and staff. Optimally, one full-time paid professional is needed for every fifteen inpatients, an equipped playroom and an ongoing allowance for toys and supplies.

Depending on the number of patients, the physical set-up of the ward and the play program staff available, activity rooms might be provided for at least four different age groups:

Infants
Toddlers
School age children
Adolescents

A separate room or area for each age level would be most beneficial, although older children often enjoy visiting and helping in the younger children's playroom. A baby in the older playroom may also be welcomed at times. In a large children's hospital, there might be a need for more than one room for the same age level.

A small hospital serving a local area may not feel it can afford a separate room for children's therapeutic activity. Any of the following might provide a temporary substitute:

—a sectioned off part of the waiting room
—a scheduled time each day in the medical classroom
—an outdoor, partially covered area
—the end of a hallway if fire regulations permit
—one end of a large patient room

There should be storage space nearby any of these areas so materials will be readily available when needed.

With or without a defined play area, an activity cart is a welcome asset. It may contain toys, games, books, records, and art and craft supplies. It could be used to deliver supplies to children in bed, to bring supplies to a play area with minimum storage space, or serve as an activity center for children in bed. If necessary, lock the cart and attach a notice announcing:

—who brings the cart to the children
—the hours of service
—who replenishes the supplies
—a diagram of where back-up items are stored

The cart could be specially designed or improvised from an existing one. Be sure that it is mobile enough to travel easily through the hall and small enough to go into patient rooms if it is to be used with children on bedrest. A cart that will only be used to deliver materials to a play area can be just shelves. If it is to serve as an activity center for bedrest patients, then drawers and work surfaces should pull through on both sides. Individual easels may also be a help.

If an inpatient play program is being developed without a playroom, use ingenuity:

—encourage children who are feeling well enough and who are in a larger room, to invite in other children
—use movable tables in the largest rooms with the most ambulatory patients
—hinge a table against the wall so that it folds up when not needed
—place beds or chairs to face one another so children can talk or play together
—invite two young children to play quietly with toys on top of one bed

–place a child-sized table and a toy shelf or drawer in patient rooms

Outpatient Play Areas

A more recently recognized area needing a planned play program and staff is the outpatient pediatric clinic. If it is not busy during open hours, it could share the time of one of the inpatient child activity workers. This sharing saves personnel costs and helps to provide coordination between the clinic and the ward, since some children move back and forth between the two. Notes kept about the reactions of a child as an inpatient will help outpatient staff members to understand his behavior when he comes to the clinic; and, conversely, misinformation or anxiety exhibited by his behavior when he is in the clinic. Try to coordinate information on patients between clinic and ward.

In a clinic, a separate room is useful for keeping track of the children, but tends to separate waiting parents from their children. This is educationally wasteful. *What happens to children when they play should be observed by parents.* They can learn how their children play alone or interact with peers. They can see the worker handling potential problems such as temper tantrums, destructive behavior, overactivity, noise or fights, and talk with her about it. They also can learn by watching the worker as she helps a child to discuss concerns or gives positive reinforcement on a job well done.

The arrangement of furniture in the clinic waiting room could help to section off an area for play. If space does not allow this, then any of the ideas suggested in the section on inpatient play areas might be tried.

Other Areas in a Medical Setting

An adult hospital having no pediatric section may have the problem of what to do with children who accompany visitors. Or, if there is an age limit for visitors in the pediatrics division, parents need a place to leave their young children while they visit a hospitalized child. Often, they leave them waiting, unsupervised, in the front lobby or waiting room. This procedure is to be avoided, for unattended and bored children can cause mischief to property, disturb and annoy others who are waiting, and often hinder traffic-flow and hospital personnel. This creates a danger to themselves and to others.

If not enough structured play is provided children will play with whatever is available, such as:

—sand-filled ash trays (as sandboxes for digging and burying treasures)
—light switches (to experiment with the power to create light and darkness and play clicking games)
—support bars along hallways (to hold onto while climbing the wall with the feet while pretending you are weightless)
—water fountains and bathroom sinks (for exploring the distance water can go)
—their own bodies (for exploration)
—buttons, ties, hooks and eyes, on clothing (for picking, twisting, swallowing)
—tissues extracted one by one from their package and dropped on the floor (to see things fly)
—fighting with other children

It is economically as well as humanely desirable to provide games, toys and supervision for active children in hospitals and clinics.

A part-time child care service can help to solve these problems. The director can explain to children, who usually are confused, why a member of the family suddenly disappeared into this huge building, what illness is, or simply what is happening. In addition, she can help adult outpatients who need help in looking after their children during their own visits to the doctor by keeping these children occupied, interested and in one safe place.

Near Admitting Office

The admitting office usually has certain times of day or days of the week which are the busiest and have the longest waiting times. A play director located near the admitting office at those times, can provide care, diversion and information to both children and parents.

Emergency Room Waiting Area

Children need supervision in the emergency room waiting area, when the waits are long and when children are often left alone in an atmosphere of acute tension. The already frayed nerves of others who are waiting become jangled by active, noisy children and tempers may flare. Instead, durable and safe toys should be available, as well as a staff member or at least a trained volunteer who can provide the benefits of supervision, human contact, information and comfort.

Pediatrician's Office

Another area where a child-oriented environment will help to relieve anxiety and promote smooth work procedures is within the pediatrician's office. Besides some small toys and art materials, the pediatrician's office could include:

- child sized table and chairs
- fish tank
- posters hung at child's level with puzzles on them to figure out
- linoleum or rug with hopscotch or checker squares on it
- small indoor slide
- wall plaques with wheels that turn or handles that move

Although children will play no matter where they are, some area should be easily identifiable as *their place to play.* At least it should be differentiated from the rest of their hospital surroundings.

Chapter 3

STAFFING A PLAY PROGRAM

The care of children in today's hospitals involves many specialists from a variety of disciplines, and it becomes increasingly clear that there is a strong need for therapeutic play personnel to help create an atmosphere in which children can learn to cope with the trauma of illness and hospitalization.

MOST PEOPLE AGREE that ill or injured children need to be prepared for coming medical events, need to have friends when left by their parents in strange surroundings, need to have sympathetic adults available when they are involved in traumatic experiences and need an opportunity to play. Play is the natural medium through which children learn about living, people and events. The difficulty in implementing those ideas, however, especially in a hospital or clinic, is to select a staff who can establish and maintain an atmosphere which provides such support to children.

The Director

Although some hospitals are satisfied with nothing more than custodial care to divert the children and prevention of accidents leading to lawsuits, most seem to want *a director who is professionally trained and who brings specialized experience to her tasks.* The background of such a director, based on the functions this person will likely have, should include:

- *Awareness* of one's own attitudes toward medical care, personnel roles in the health sciences and patient's rights. Continuing exploration of one's motivation and the effects of one's own previous medical experiences.

–*Course work* in the study of the child from birth to maturity in all his physical, emotional, adaptive, perceptual, cognitive and social and family aspects. An understanding of the impact of illness and disability on children and their families together with knowledge of adaptations that can be effective.

–*A repertoire* of crafts, expressive media, ideas for dramatization and ideas for incorporating learning experiences into play.

–Past *experience* with children for the much-needed inner confidence that invites respect from others. Any experience in group leadership of children is helpful and the work involved in nursery schools, public and private schools, classes for exceptional children, tutoring of children with special problems or camp counseling with special groups is especially helpful.

–*Organizational and planning ability* to be able to formulate short and long-range goals and smooth administrative tangles.

–*Teaching ability,* not only to teach the children, but to convey child development issues and child care goals to community people, to other health care workers and to parents.

Programs tend to develop in the direction of the background and interests of the staff. From what fields of work do play directors come? This varies from one hospital to another, if such workers are employed at all. Among the professional backgrounds from which current leaders of therapeutic play programs come are: child development, social work, recreation therapy, public or private school teaching, nursery school teaching, occupational therapy, psychology, sociology and nursing. As a result of varied emphasis in different hospitals even the titles of program leaders across the country vary. There are titles such as: play director, child activity director, therapist, recreation director, child life director, play lady, toy lady, child development specialist, play specialist and preparation specialist. Because there are overlapping competencies in the health and social science fields, there are differing points of view in each.

To find a professional staff, send notices of the individuals needed to colleges and universities, community colleges that offer degrees in the fields mentioned and to professional journals and associations.

When interviewing job applicants, find out what areas of specialization they can offer. Decide whether the education, experience and interests offered will work into the goals of the program. Help her or him to understand what has already been established as program objectives (either by other professional interviews, the first play director, or by the established play program staff interviewing for program expansion) and ask questions as to whether the applicant feels able to contribute towards those objectives.

Once a program has begun, the director could begin a handbook describing the job and a reference list of specific staff departments and organizations that contribute to the functioning of the program. Such a handbook could prove invaluable in maintaining steady growth of the program.

The newly hired play director may be responsible for most of her own training. One must guard, however, against the temptation to immediately implement ideas before taking a more careful look at the given situation. In the long run there is more benefit in taking time in the beginning to:

—observe other staff and gain an understanding and appreciation of their particular jobs
—meet current staff and share ideas about how they view her new job position
—get to know specific staff, departments and outside organizations that support the program
—observe the total ward or clinic routine so that there is a better understanding of the patients' experiences
—learn the already established channels of giving and receiving information on patients and think of how to become involved in this way
—spend time organizing the play and office area
—set up regular meeting times with supportive personnel who will give constructive feedback on the progress of the program

Although the above does require an initial expenditure of time along with regular follow-up, it has proved to be a time saver and an effective tool for program growth.

The direction the program takes may be influenced by the source of funding. Sometimes the decision to strive toward one goal or another is made for the director. If pediatric nurses provide the impetus for hiring a play director, for example, then their needs may have to have highest priority, at least at the start. They may be hoping the director can take children, whose behavior is causing them problems, off their hands. This goal may be broadened by aiming to share the work involved in assessing why a particular child behaves in ways unacceptable to them and what can be done together to improve the situation. Nurses may feel remorse at having to leave young patients who need their attention when they are needed for more critical cases. Showing appreciation for their referrals and keeping them informed of progress while welcoming their help whenever their time permits, creates good will.

The volunteer auxiliary may sponsor a play director's salary, but even in hospitals which have little money, this arrangement should be only on a demonstration or temporary basis. The support of special items is always welcome but an effective play director is as essential to the young patient's recovery as other team specialists. Because physical therapists, inhalation therapists, medical social workers and other health specialists are not subsidized by private fund-raising, neither should play program staff be—although many a fine program may have *begun* that way. Some directors of hospital volunteer programs have placed volunteers in pediatric settings for years but have unsuccessfully tried to involve hospital staff in training or supervision of them. A professional play director employed through the auxiliary will likely spend at least part of her time in such training and supervision.

While the training and direction of volunteers can be an important part of running an effective therapeutic play program, the activities they are trained to engage in and the amount of time devoted to their supervision must be related to the carefully considered goals for the program.

Social work departments may have in mind a director-therapist who works in play and in discussion groups, who involves parents in their children's progress and who coordinates her work well with the total health care staff.

Eventually, a play program should exist on its own, as a Child Life and Education Unit, Child Activity Program or the Play Department. Even then, the original sponsoring department could remain advisory.

To become a separately funded program, keep hospital administrators informed, either directly or through other staff members, of the benefits and services that the therapeutic play program provides. Since medical directors and budget analysts make judgments and give advice as to where the monies available can best be spent, they need to be knowledgeable. Private groups, medical auxiliaries or guilds and other community groups also may be interested.

Even after the program is established, staff hired and services begun, continued justification is required in some medical settings. Use all of the help that can be obtained to counteract the tendency to diminish or freeze the financial assistance previously given to the program.

Communication with the department heads in pediatrics, psychiatry, nursing, radiology, surgery or food services can facilitate formation of an advisory committee. This committee might meet several times a year to coordinate the developments in children's services. It can also facilitate needed changes through the relevant authority of the membership or by their communication with the hospital director on the program's behalf. If budget cuts or restrictions are suggested in departmental meetings, committee members who are present can stand up for the program and provide leadership to the others. In some hospitals this need is filled by the patient care or patient relations committees.

When a play program staff is small, or there is only one staff member, decisions about which aspect of the work has priority will affect the children directly. This needs to be a purposeful choice and should not be left to tradition, accident or circumstance.

Suppose, for example, it is decided to start by establishing an inpatient playroom, play and direct daily activities there and report observations to the staff. The items purchased, the schedule followed, the effect on the children will be much different than if it had been decided instead to establish working relationships with administrators and other staff to change the physical environment and climate of the hospital, or to embark on a series of sessions designed for nurses, doctors, volunteers or others on children's psychological reactions to medical care.

If the choice is to work with individual children as much as possible, the need to maintain the cleanliness and safety of the play area will prove hampering unless there are sufficient arrangements with housekeeping or supply personnel.

While engaged in an eager campaign to affect attitudes about children in a medical setting, the director will be seen by some as neglecting direct work with the children whom they consider more important.

In any case, the decision to pursue one series of tasks rather than another needs to be carefully thought out. One full-time staff person could not do justice to both orientations. When more than one person is available to help, of course, more tasks can be carried out more effectively and efficiently with multiple direct benefits to the children.

Job Guidelines

There are as yet no uniformly accepted descriptions of job duties. Besides, patients in hospitals and clinics have varied needs.

Consider these differing goals and decide the priorities in the specific setting for the particular patients:

- –improve the hospital atmosphere so that children will feel more comfortable and less anxious
- –organize informal health education sessions
- –coordinate children's play with the educational program of the teacher sent by the public schools
- –conduct group projects and crafts sessions
- –familiarize each child with admission and treatment procedures so that they are better prepared
- –have play situations that strengthen certain muscle groups and develop neuromuscular growth
- –fill the playroom shelves with toys from which the children can be free to choose

—organize individual play sessions with each child, with consultation from the psychiatrist
—observe and report significant behavior of the child
—correlate own work with children with that of the team

How should one decide which goals to pursue? On the basis of one's specialized training? Or on what the children in that setting need? Is it possible to accomplish every proposed goal?

But is there one right way? No, there are many avenues to reaching children. The one to choose depends on:

NEED:	what mental health services are missing that are needed?
IMMEDIACY:	what can be started now? which goals are most likely to be supported by the pediatric and nursing staff, and by administrators?
GOALS:	how do current actions fit into long-term plans for a therapeutic play program?

Cooperation With Others

Staff play program personnel must cooperate with each other and win cooperation from other staff members in order to have a successful interdisciplinary approach to a child's overall care and well-being.

Each person who comes into planned contact with pediatric patients through the auspices of the play program should have some understanding of how his work fits into the general plan and what would be helpful to it in terms of schedule, preparation and content. Then, whenever possible, try to evaluate this effort soon afterward, so that the person who gave it will understand why the children were receptive or were unresponsive and in what way his comments, interactions or demonstration eased their concerns or answered their questions.

Even staff people, experts in their own fields and knowledgeable about the program may need some help in planning their role:

—A nurse could teach new mothers about sleeping, language and play of babies in their first year, but she may be helped by knowing the kinds of questions parents have been asking and she may wish to borrow suitable toys for demonstration from the playroom collection. Cooperation will help everyone.

—A physician who has the time and interest to discuss drug abuse with preteens will want to know how long to talk, whether to have a question/answer session or show a film. Tell him to ask the youngsters!

—A lab technician who can show and explain equipment for blood drawing needs to know the fears young children have expressed and what particular laboratory items it would be most helpful to discuss. (Usually they are the ones that are most visible during the blood drawing: the syringe, needle, tourniquet, tubes, slides and microscope.)

—A nurse may be more helpful than the play director in bringing small groups of children on fifteen minute tours of the examining or treatment room area. But she is even more effective if the play director first alerts her to the comments the children made that revealed their concerns about shots, restraints or undressing.

—A staff dentist or dental hygienist may be willing to help teach toothbrushing to a group of youngsters waiting in the clinic, bringing along brushes and toothpaste. But he needs guidance to insure that his talk is understood by the children, is not too long and that he does not insist that older children demonstrate their toothbrushing "in front of everyone."

The more staff who participates, the more effective the program will be, provided their participation is appropriate to the chosen goals and methods. Their contribution will also have the effect of making them more alert to the psychological effect of procedures on children.

Parents

Try especially hard to involve the parents of the pediatric patients. Loving and knowledgeable parents can ease the pain of an ill child's spirit as well as comfort his body. *However, parents need clarification of their role in the medical setting.*

If parents are welcome in the playroom, they will join in activities with their child. Sometimes the art, craft or messy media being used proves as successful in relaxing a parent under stress as it does the child! (A one-page handout could be given to parents stating the benefits and a description of projects which could be duplicated at home.)

Parents will also raise more questions about child-rearing problems when they feel free to enter into the activities. Some questions can be referred to the doctors, others can be answered but noted for future reference as a possible concern of the mother. Occasionally, such questions indicate a need to refer the parents to the social worker for more intensive or long-term help.

After parents feel comfortable in the playroom they might be asked to help with other children besides their own, or to help watch for safety and comfort factors in the playroom while staff members are visiting a child who is on bedrest. Besides the assistance such help gives, parents say that it helps *them*. It takes their minds off their own worries, occupies their idle time while their own child is busy with a procedure and helps them to feel useful at a time when many of their normal parental responsibilities have been taken away from them by hospital personnel or rules.

Once parents become known to the staff and feel they can reach them, many will also offer help in the maintenance and upkeep of the program. For this purpose, keep in mind nondemanding projects that require help from others such as rolling yarn into balls, putting a new wagon together, changing the aquarium, mending doll clothes and puppets or labeling new toys.

Patients

One of the best sources of help in a therapeutic play program is the pediatric patient himself. Enlist the aid and advice of the patient. They can help each other in many ways:

—A child who is convalescing may be able to comfort a newly admitted child. He sometimes has insight into another child's feelings much sooner than busy adults do.

—Teenage patients may want to help plan their own activities or volunteer with those of younger children.

—Sisters or brothers who arrive together as patients can help one another and help staff to know the other's needs.

—A child who speaks both English and another language may make an excellent translator for another child who only speaks that language.
—Children will happily add to the posted list, "What Toys Do We Need?"
—They make good reporters for the children's newspaper.
—They like to wash dishes, dolls and doll clothes, to scrub table tops and easels, and to shine sinks.

Students

In a teaching hospital, there are likely some students who are training in pediatrics, nursing and social work. As their instructors recognize that there is a worthwhile, established program, they will probably wish to utilize its play areas as a place for their students to observe child behavior and will donate hours to your program.

If the hospital is not affiliated with an educational institution, ask the administrator's help in contacting teachers from neighboring colleges. Try the college departments of psychology, social work, home economics, child development, public health, sociology, education, special education, recreation or physical education, art and music. Offer their students field work experience in return for help. Be prepared to give a description of the job the student will carry out and to state how supervision or information sessions will be provided. Not only will students have a chance to observe the normally developing characteristics of children in play sessions, they may also be able to sustain a long-term project. They can:

—collect research data
—teach several health and self-care sessions
—maintain and use supplies on a play cart for bed patients
—help gather and post health education materials for parents

Students are especially important if you are working in a facility without a volunteer department.

Use all the human resources available to provide regular, consistent, trained help for children.

Chapter 4

RECRUITING AND TRAINING PLAY PROGRAM VOLUNTEERS

Volunteers, nonpaid people from the community who commit their energy and time to regular hours of child care in the hospital, are invaluable to a play program. But the success of their earnest and dedicated efforts will depend on an effective program of selection and training.

VOLUNTEERS FROM THE COMMUNITY can offer direct help to children and they can provide many needed and diverse services such as:

films
animal care
company at meals
filing
help with picnic
instrumental music
inventory
observations
photography
shopping
escorting
typing

They can also build and repair:
flannel boards
boxes with different textures to feel
scrapbooks with articles on child development
materials for child to make greeting cards

- structures for sand and water play
- puppets
- yard equipment
- blocks
- housekeeping corner
- puppet theater

Create:

- a patient lending library and bookmobile cart
- small bedside toys
- infant mobiles
- song fests
- bulletin boards
- posters
- holiday gifts
- newspaper with the children
- tray favors

Collect:

- books
- puzzles
- large cartons
- collage materials
- old decks of cards
- containers for storage
- scrap fabrics and trim
- ingredients for homemade clay

Talk:

- with parents about a successful event or craft
- with non-English speaking families, translate for parents and siblings
- with community service groups
- with new volunteers to help orient them
- with siblings of patients who are with the doctor
- with child on preadmission tour or puppet show
- with child waiting to be seen by doctor, and tell or read stories
- with child on missing school work and tutor

with child of adult outpatients
with child of visitors to patients

If the volunteer knows the specific job he is depended upon to do and is prepared for it, he is likely to be more reliable than a person who feels he can be easily replaced. Rewards through tangible recognitions such as badges, pins and certificates given by the volunteer services division are one way to say "Thank you" to valuable volunteers. But the volunteer may appreciate even more the sure knowledge he can have that he has done well a specific job directly beneficial to children. The verbalization of appreciation for a job well-done is one of the director's most important jobs.

Where can volunteers be found? If there is a separate office of Volunteer Services, let the director know how many volunteers are needed, what they will do and what training will be provided. Then she can have the program needs in mind as she interviews potential volunteers.

On what basis should volunteers be accepted? It seems more important to accept them on the basis of their warm feelings for children, their reliability and their willingness to learn than on the basis of their age, experience or previous training.

Having specific requirements may lead to difficulties. For example, if the preference is for the services of adult women experienced in rearing children, the volunteer may be mature, wise, dependable, reassuring and comforting. But she may also be opinionated, inflexible and unwilling to learn!

Each individual must be considered individually. Work-study students or high school students can offer sparkle, energy, contemporary attitudes and a willingness to try new ideas. Or they could be glib, interested only in sociality and always late. While college students can assist testing theories in practice and challenging staff to explain their thinking they can also limit themselves to fulfilling only the minimum requirements needed to pass a field work course.

If no volunteer services exist, assistance will be needed in finding some helpers. Try to find trained teachers, recreation leaders, retired social workers, former instructors in education, nurses working only part-time. They have a special body of knowledge and may be experienced with children. Recruit a few volunteers to do the calling, posting of notices, sending of letters. Use these volunteers to help train other, less experienced persons.

Be enthusiastic in your recruiting. Speak about this in every meeting you attend and with every visitor. Post a notice on your own bulletin boards and on employee boards as well. Send notices also to your local and city newspapers; letters to the editor; to clubs for senior citizens, for teens, for service groups such as Legion, Sertoma, Business Women's Association, senior Scouts and Horizon Club; and to public and private high schools. Call City Hall to find out if your city has a central clearing house for volunteer activities, sometimes called a Volunteer Bureau. Call large businesses and inquire if they permit time off for charitable services of employees. You may find low-income workers trying to upgrade their skills in government-sponsored programs and the U.S. Department of Labor sponsors work-incentive programs about which you should inquire. Be inventive and persevere.

HOW TO UTILIZE VOLUNTEER GROUPS EFFECTIVELY

Once there is a volunteer staff, what is to be done with them? How can they be trained and organized?

Orientation

Many hospitals using the services of volunteers offer them a general lecture and a tour of the facility. The volunteer learns the rules about uniforms, about keeping information confidential and about protecting the patient's privacy. Follow up this kind of orientation by giving more specific information and developing the confidence of the volunteer. They want to know: How do I do my job? How will I know if I am doing the right thing? How can I avoid harming the patient? How do I cope with difficult situations? Some direct answers can be given, but to involve them in a lasting learning process, try encouraging discussion of these questions. Choose a specific situation or event to discuss. To create an even more personal atmosphere, group the volunteers in threes so that every one has a chance to talk.

Handbook

Where there are volunteers, there are often volunteer handbooks. They generally give a welcome, some idea of the hospital's purpose and departments and suggestions on being an ethical, responsible volunteer.

If many volunteers are to be involved it may be worth the time to create additional information sheets on:

—volunteering in the clinic
—volunteering in the ward
—helping new patients, etc.

Preservice Training

A week of daily sessions can be offered on such topics as:

—how to select appropriate toys
—how to present creative materials
—how to watch and write about children's behavior

A brief overview for the volunteer followed by some practice time in actually setting up the playroom, trying out toys and creative media and meeting the staff is valuable. To generate lively discussions invite questions arising out of their need to know rather than the leader's need to tell.

Remember to:

—Define how long the session can run, where it will be held, what time and how many will likely be there.

—Give help during the session, if necessary, by asking relevant questions, encouraging the volunteers to comment and otherwise taking part.

Afterwards, discuss what happened. Although volunteers may not have much experience in working with children, they often have good ideas about making hospital care more humane. Listen as well as lecture.

Use various specialized personnel to conduct the sessions in therapeutic play with children, creative media, observation methods and psychology.

When you use the services of various staff members to lead training sessions, no staff person should have to give more than an hour or two a year to the project. It does demand, however, that the staff member has to think generally about services to children and particularly about the liaison between himself or his department and the play program. In addition, in planning his part, the staff member should preferably meet with the director or at least have a telephone conversation. As he becomes more aware of the program, new opportunities for the children of both divisions served may result.

> A new speech therapist discussed children's speech development with one group. Two astute volunteers asked how speech problems can be detected in children as they play. With a new realization of the possible help a volunteer could give in screening for problems, he invited their observation of him with children at play. After having been taught several ways to spot delayed speech and articulation errors, volunteers in the pediatric clinic playroom could then alert the play director, who in turn could document the speech or language level of the child at that time, possibly leading to a referral.

"Scavenger Hunt"

Because most people feel more comfortable in new situations if they are encouraged to observe first, before "doing," each volunteer should have at least one day devoted to this in the medical setting at the beginning of his service. The volunteer should not feel rushed, but should know he is expected to absorb information and the "atmosphere."

Some people, eager to help sick children, jump right into situations before they have begun to understand what is going on. This means that weeks later, they may discover they have been working against the goals of the program rather than towards them.

It also means that if they did not spend time initially learning particulars about housekeeping chores such as what supplies are available and where they are located, unnecessary amounts of the staff's time will be taken up later answering such questions.

In addition, during orientation, volunteers receive much new information, but it may not be clear then to the program director or to the volunteer just how much of this was meaningful and will be remembered. Seeing what the volunteer has written on the Scavenger Hunt list can help to check on the acquisition of concepts and facts. It can also assist the director in assessing the volunteer's strengths and limitations. (One volunteer, for instance, may show aptness in observing children's behavior while another exhibits creative ideas for activities with children.)

Each Scavenger Hunt would have to be adapted to particular programs in relation to what is considered important, but typical questions might range from:

—How can you tell if it is all right for a child to get out of bed and come to the playroom?

—What is the name of the head nurse and what is her job?

to:

—Where are the puzzles stored?

—Where can the key to the storage closet be found?

Rounds and Shifts

Rather than allowing volunteers to wander freely in and out, have them arrive in shifts. They can then be distributed at times when the children need them the most. In addition, when the time the volunteers will come is known, plans can be made to start them off together. A meeting, called rounds, can be held at the start of each shift. These are short sessions in which the plans for the day are briefly outlined and specific jobs or leadership roles are identified and assigned. Brief background is given about those children who will especially need attention. Such meetings give volunteers up-to-date information and provides continuity for the children. In addition, volunteers can discuss experiences from the last time they worked and make plans for improving the ways and the environment in which they work with children.

For example, one group of volunteers, meeting with the play director, compiled this list from their own experiences of giving verbal directions:

Not Helpful	*Helpful*
"Don't get your hands dirty!"	"It's okay to get paint on your hands. You have a plastic apron on and we can wash your hands later."
"No! No! No! Don't do that!"	"We only put *food* into the hamster's cage (and remove

	child's hand from cage)." or "Shall we take the hamster out of his cage for a while and pet him?"
"Why don't you talk to me?"	"Sometimes children don't like to talk to new people. You can talk to me when you're ready."
"Get away from there!"	"The water fountain is just for drinking, not for playing."
"Stop grabbing toys."	"John needs that truck he is playing with. Let's find another for you." or "Let's see if John needs a garage for his truck. We can use the blocks."
"You're a bad boy!"	"It hurts Susie when you hit her. Use your words to tell her what you need."
"Stop crying! It's not that important."	"You worked hard to get all the pegs in the board and then they fell. Do you want some help to pick them up?"

Discussion Groups

When volunteers express the need to know more about a particular idea or job, they are likely to attend a session arranged on that topic. Adults need to react, to apply theory to their personal experiences and to ask questions in order to learn. They learn more when they are involved in choosing the topic and entering into a self-teaching process.

For example, in a discussion of the impact of hospitalization on children, ask group members to write briefly about their earliest remembered medical experience. Use these examples, anonymously, to point out the effects of stress on children, the memory of painful or pleasant medical events and the benefits of personal care and consideration.

In a session on talking with parents of sick children, ask the group to discuss their own feelings about visits to a doctor's office for a check-up or treatment. They may recall such feelings as: fear of the diagnosis, confusion over the doctor's instructions, concern about children left at home, anger at having to wait and worry about cost. These are easily empathized and extended when the obvious analogies between themselves and the parents are drawn.

Workshops

Experiencing the same materials that the child will use personalizes them. Using fingerpaint, crafts or construction materials all help in giving the volunteer confidence that he can create inviting media sessions with children.

Improvising their own simple toys to use with children demonstrates to volunteers that materials need not be complicated or purchased commercially to be effective:

snowflakes: from folded torn paper
tic-tac-toe: paper and pencil or chalk and slate
finger puppet: tear two holes for walking fingers near rim of upturned paper cup
tongue blade or popsicle stick: draw face on end

Remembering their own childhood games can help volunteers feel that improvising games with children is still in style. They do not always need to rely on specific toys or the playroom. Divide the group of learners into pairs. Ask them to write down every game they can remember that requires at least two persons but no equipment, no pencil, paper or props. In the sharing session that follows, the group will surprise themselves with the long lists of all the games they had forgotten they knew!

Bulletin Boards

Bulletin boards give people a warm, neighborhood feeling of sharing and they are usually gathering places for volunteers. Have one for the playroom volunteers and include on it:

Meetings you can attend:	film series, special speakers, demonstrations of techniques, television closed circuit showing, open staff meetings, grand rounds.
Craft ideas:	list items needed, use a picture of the craft to show how it is done, say why or when to use it. A volunteer could devise a series of these to alternate.
HELP!	one-time jobs that need to be done soon, or regular assignments that need to be filled, scrapcraft materials that need to be saved.
About the program:	one-page information sheets with photos or drawings, newspaper clippings or articles about your program or other related programs, annual reports of the hospital or at least the section about the play program's services, sample forms that are used to observe behavior or describe techniques.

Keep in mind that anything you post may also be read by staff, parents and older children.

Self-teaching

If no one can be there to meet with or observe the volunteer, encourage the use of self-teaching materials.

—A tape recorder, for example, can be useful when the volunteer is evaluating a specific project.

One student volunteer who was learning to encourage children's dramatizations of doctors and nurses at work, heard later on the tape playback the many times she kept repeating to the child, "Ok, now what?" It had been difficult for her to bear the silences while the child thought.

She also heard herself interrupt the child's spontaneous verbal description of imagined surgery and recovery by interjecting questions prematurely and responding unnecessarily with, "Oh, that's interesting," and "Oh, really?" Listening to the recording was self-corrective, the student reported in a note to the play director.

—A television kinescope of an event helps the volunteers in a large university center to develop a perspective on room arrangements, socialization of children with the staff, actions that facilitated and those that temporarily blocked children's efforts and responses.

Volunteer assistance in the play program can be critically needed, but the volunteer who performs significant services to children deserves the support of the staff in this demanding and important work. Back them up with specific training and supportive supervision.

Chapter 5

ORGANIZING A PLAYROOM

The organization of the playroom and its materials can be as individual and ingenious as the personality and ability of the play director and playroom staff. Just as a home can be organized casually or strictly depending on the taste and requirements of the family who lives there, so the playroom should reflect the priorities of the people who are working in it and of the children who need their care. There are some basic limitations of space, equipment, budget and storage facilities which each program must work around, but they should not restrict the primary goal of the program: to help children cope with the possible traumas of being in a medical setting.

SPACE

Define Space

THE FIRST STEP in deciding what equipment and supplies to obtain for your therapeutic play program is to analyze the space you have. If there is not a specific room already set aside for play, an area will have to be "defined." This can be done with:

–A rug placed at the end of the hallway, away from traffic and elevators, can indicate the boundaries of the play area and so create your "playroom"

–An arrangement of screen dividers or benches can designate the play area and provide recognizable boundaries for children

–Child-sized domestic furniture can be placed at one end of a carpeted waiting room and toys can be available as needed from a cupboard on wheels

Create Space

Even if an area is designated entirely for play, it may not be large enough for your play program needs. To gain more space for activity, try these ideas:

—Attach a painting easel at a slight angle to the wall (so that a chair can be brought up to it)

—Suspend a book rack with four sides from the ceiling in a corner (leaving space below for soft chairs)

—Attach the door of cabinet on a piano hinge (so that it can be lifted up and used as a tabletop for board games)

—Cut a hole in the countertop next to the sink (so that used paper towels and trash can be poked through the slot and dropped into a receptacle, thereby avoiding a tip-over trash barrel taking up limited floor space)

—Use the same notion for a toy-bin, to encourage children to return toys. (A hole in another cabinet drops into a plastic basket. Each morning, a volunteer empties it and returns toys to shelf)

—Stabilize the door to the playroom in an open position, making an "L" and behind it, an interest corner. (Hang up an unbreakable mirror behind it and you have the start of a "home" corner)

—Hinge the puppet theater to fold flat against the wall when not in use (Storing puppets on individual pegs inside the theater walls, saving storage space.)

—Put wheels on the toy shelves (to move them where needed or to temporarily store them elsewhere if the playroom is needed for bed patients)

—Keep the phonograph in an office or storage room adjacent to the playroom with only the speakers or headphones available in the playroom. (Save playroom shelf space and relieve worry about tiny hands playing with the dials, buttons and records.)

—Attach plaques to the wall with wheels that turn, gears that mesh, tiny doors that open, etc., thereby creating stand-up "busy areas." (They can be made from Busy Box, Whirl-a-Gear or from hardware accessories)

—"Paint" shapes on the floor with tape or chalk to offer hopscotch and other sidewalk action games that can be played in a limited area.

Utilize Space

If there is the unusual luxury of ample space for a pediatric patient's playroom, there are great opportunities for success: space for play vehicles, toys and supplies and space for beds, allowing wheelchairs and wagons to be brought in and nonambulatory patients to be part of the playroom group.

The space savers previously mentioned may still be used, but with generous floor space many of the following activities and facilities could be added.

—Centers of interest: such as a housekeeping corner, block corner, "doctor's office," giving the children a wide selection of "places to visit."

—A large central activity table, offering relatively structured play for those who need ideas or those who want to produce a handcraft product.

—Displays of children's work.

—Convenient storage for large items near the play area.

—A sink and work counter at a child's elbow level, helping to encourage cleanliness and making possible such activities as painting, pasting and clay work.

—Windows and window sills, possibly providing open atmosphere, natural lighting and places for plants to grow.

—Floor surfaces (which can be easily washed or vacuumed) and bare enough and warm enough to sit or lie down on.

—An observation room with a one-way mirror adjoining the playroom, making it possible for staff and students to watch without disturbing the children.

Evaluate the Area

Look over the entire play area and answer these questions: a) Does each section welcome? b) Does it suggest its function by its arrangement and contents? c) Are there few enough items in it to be clear and discrete? d) Are there enough toys, games or materials to make play productive?

Look at each wall, then at the furniture or equipment against it. Do your posters, children's pictures or other hanging objects make sense with the items nearby?

Is the sink easy to reach from the area where messy or

creative play is done? Are the towels low enough for a child to reach one easily? Can a wheelchair patient reach the faucets?

Some items belong together and should be clustered. Are all the animals, science display materials and related posters displayed together or are they scattered throughout the room? Are the domestic play furniture, dress-up clothes and mirror together?

Are things convenient? Cleaning supplies kept in locked boxes in several areas may make clean-up quicker. Although the bookcase may be in a corner of the room, the book-return box may be located near or even outside of the playroom door for quick return and retrieval of books.

Will the room be left open after the regular supervised play program hours? It is much easier for the play director if she can lock the door in her absence. She does not have to leave a totally safe environment that way and when she returns, she does not have to invest a lot of time cleaning up from the activity during her absence. It also means, however, that unless there are relay shifts of play personnel to unlock the door and supervise activity at night and on weekends, the children will be denied the use of the playroom during those periods. Perhaps a system can be designed in which the room is always available even if it means that most toys are put away when there is no supervision and some children could "check out" toys to use while the play director is gone. Perhaps a cupboard with toys and supplies may be left open to volunteers, students, nurses or parents.

Equipment and Supplies

After considering the selection and organization of a play area, decide on the kinds of supplies and equipment needed for a therapeutic play program. Many play directors, staff personnel and experienced volunteers will have their needs and resources well in mind. However, for those less experienced or just setting up, there are many resource books listing standard supplies used in children's programs. In the hospital, you may be able to order many of the expendables through the hospital storehouse. They are not only more accessible there, they may also be less expensive to your budget than when purchased outside. For example:

- wide paper on a roll
- carbon paper
- clip boards
- colored chalk
- colored note cards
- colored transparent tabs
- crayons
- fine point felt pens
- glue
- lined note pads
- manila folders
- notebook paper
- paper clips
- newsprint paper
- cotton
- tongue depressors
- paper punch
- pencils
- rubber bands
- rulers
- scissors — adult
- scissors — child
- shaving cream
- staples
- stationery
- three-ring binders
- thumb tacks
- white pipe cleaners
- paper cutter
- tape
- gauze

In addition, ill or handicapped children *need:*

–Wagons for transporting patients who are on bed rest or who need to go a long distance for an activity such as a picnic.

–Lap boards that fit over arms of wheelchairs with half-circle-cutout for patient and built-up sides to keep toys or food from sliding off.

–Sand and water tables at a height that children can stand next to, or wheelchairs can wheel up to.

–Standard sun umbrellas or awnings to protect children in the yard from hot sun or warm drizzles.

–Clip-on umbrellas for beds and wheelchairs.

Free Materials

Besides providing many of the materials that need to be purchased, the hospital can provide a treasure of scrap materials.

Play personnel can gain cooperation from employees in various departments. Thus, besides having saved expenses by gathering free materials, more people will have been enlisted in support of the goals of the program.

The following partial list gives an idea of what can often be obtained without cost around a medical facility:

—From Carpentry: wood scraps, sandpaper

—From Animal Care: animals, food, sawdust, cages, veterinary services

—From Dietary: oatmeal boxes, egg cartons, crates, cans, supplies for play dough and baking, foil dishes, extra large cans for storage

—From Telephone Repair Men: telephone wire for stringing and making jewelry, old telephones

—From the Gift Shop: cigar boxes, small containers to cover with contact paper and use for building blocks, Christmas cards and catalogs to make informational scrapbooks

—From the Receiving Department: packing materials, large cartons, cardboard sheets, styrofoam

—From Volunteers, Parents and Staff: yarn, material scraps, plastic containers, old playing cards, thread spools, dress trimmings, buttons, pie tins

—From the Mail Room: empty spools from cord, cancelled stamps, stampers no longer used

—From the Linen Room: old sheets for Halloween costumes and tie dyeing, doctors' worn coats for dramatic play, children's worn pajamas for puppet clothes

—From Radiology: used, reject, blank x-rays for children to draw own x-rays; used reject x-rays of body parts for teaching children the kind of pictures that will be taken

–From the Equipment Storeroom: old storage shelves, office equipment, x-ray light for "the doctor corner"

–From the Pharmacy: pill boxes, plastic bottles

In return, let the children show their appreciation to their friends. Besides showing appreciation, this will provide creative activities for the children.

–Thank you notes to the cook who saved oatmeal boxes so they could make drums.
–Cookies baked especially for the repairman who used his lunch hour to hammer a nail hole into each of a hundred bottle caps so they could be strung.
–An article in the children's newspaper describing the picnic arranged by the dietary staff.

To Make

A third source of supplies is those interested people or volunteer organizations who offer to make things for the program. They usually ask what they can do and their help can be put to the best use if the list of needs is kept up-to-date. They should get into the habit of checking what is needed rather than going ahead on their own projects, so that every volunteer donation is V.I.P. (Very Important for the Playroom) instead of being a duplicate. Some examples are:

finger puppets
hand puppets
punching bags
stitchery kits
bean bags
cloth animals
cloth dolls
collage kits
door decorating kits
dresses and T-shirts for patient to wear
plastic aprons for children and volunteers
wooden miniatures of hospital apparatus

STORAGE

Location

To help children maintain spontaneity and interest in a project, needed supplies should be near or in the playroom area. When either a child or a group leader needs to travel to the far end of the ward or clinic to obtain needed materials, involvement or motivation may be lost along with a lot of time.

Amount

Although storage space is needed for expendable supplies such as clay and paint, storage requirements need to be kept to a minimum in a hospital or clinic. This prevents the "pack-rat" syndrome or building up a nest of items that may prove useful "someday." Keep the inventory current and manageable. Let the hospital's storerooms hold certain supplies, just ordering them on a regular basis. Standing orders can be left for paper, foods, linens and office supplies.

Organization

Before organizing the storage of your play program, consider the needs of those who will be using them. For instance, if volunteers will be setting up activities with children, be more specific in labeling supplies than if the director were the only one drawing from the supply closet. (Items get returned more easily if the shelf is marked with the same label as the box of material.)

If the play director or one experienced person will be supervising materials most of the time, storage can be organized by materials, (such as paper on one shelf, paints on another, etc.) This saves energy because you can store more of the same items together with one label. It also gives you a chance to be more flexible with the storage and assortment of materials. In addition, you can clearly see your inventory and ordering needs.

Collect quantities of various kinds of containers and use them! They help to keep materials organized: Some examples to store construction toys and large items are:

–Plastic dishpans – they are strong, easily stacked, can be wiped clean and can be brought to a bed patient

—Five gallon ice cream cartons covered with contact paper
—Large metal containers from shortening or flour; (talk with the cook or head of dietary to obtain them). These work well for bulk supplies such as wood scraps, packing material and sawdust

Supplies can be organized by activity. (This works best when the materials will be used by people who have not had experience in starting and maintaining activities.) In other words, one container would hold all the materials needed for one activity. Be sure to include directions for the activity on a card in each container! You can take this whole "activity container" to a bed patient without fuss or bother. Some examples of containerized activities are:

—Clay and shapes for imprinting it
—Lanyard hooks, plastic thread, instruction book, blunt scissors
—Burlap squares, yarn, blunt needles with large holes
—Stamp pads, stampers with designs, dates, department names, form and paper
—Collage scraps with cardboard and paste
—Paper dolls, fold-up paper furniture, blunt scissors
—Lightweight wood scraps and glue

This method necessitates periodic inventory checks to see that activity containers are complete and neat.

Clear organization of a playroom and its supplies facilitates the work of the staff and the children. It is well worth the effort involved in designing a plan for it.

Chapter 6

PROVIDING THERAPEUTIC ACTIVITIES

The types of activities which can be incorporated in a play program are as varied as the minds of children. In this chapter, a number of activities are described which have been proven to work well in a medical setting. They can serve as guidelines for a new program or as source material for ongoing programs looking for activities to meet special needs. Although activities have been arbitrarily grouped it is important to remember that there exists an overlapping.

Dramatic Play

CHILDREN LIKE TO PLAY-ACT even when they are hospitalized and they will reenact illnesses and accidents or anticipate medical procedures through dramatics. "You be the patient," they say, "I'll be the doctor and check you." or "You must be the mama and I'll be the baby who cries."

Through such play-acting, the child can release his fears, frustrations, tensions and anger. By acting out medical situations of which he may become a part, the hospitalized or ill child will begin to understand them and later gain control over his fear of them. As he pretends to draw blood, take blood pressure, give spinal taps, he becomes better able afterwards to tolerate these procedures on himself.

This kind of play is enhanced with the addition of props, such as:

—Puppets: heads for them can be salvaged from dolls. Then, wrap a cloth around the neck piece to cover the hand that will hold it.

—Finger puppets: a cloth over the child's finger and draw features with a felt marker pen.

—Doctor bags: with real instruments and a generous supply of expendable supplies such as tape, bandages, face masks, paper hats, tongue blades, etc. are useful props for medical dramatics. On a sheet on the table, place a large doll, a few instruments and hospital clothing. Leave the doctor bag open so the "audience" can see the other contents.

—A miniature hospital (like a doll's house) with patient rooms, X-ray area, labs, treatment room, operating room, kitchen, bathrooms and playrooms becomes an excellent "stage" for these dramas.

—Doll figures representing families, as well as hospital staff, should be in proportion to the furniture in the doll's house. Furniture can be made from cardboard and fabric but wood furniture is sturdier and longer lasting.

—Washable plastic doll furniture can be transformed into hospital furniture by such methods as pasting buttons on chair sides to create wheelchairs.

—Miniature models of equipment such as an X-ray table or heart catheterization machine can be used in dramatization with a doll to help children prepare for the real event or to understand it afterwards.

—Washable dress-up clothes in children's sizes, that slip on and off easily encourage role-playing. Three that are popular are a skirt made of one fabric piece, sewn on the side, with an elastic waistband; and a one-piece vest, sewn at the shoulders, opening in front, decorated with large buttons; and a doctor's coat.

—Add accessories such as hats, ties, jewelry, adult shoes, purses and wallets. Clothing items can be stored in a suitcase, hung on clothes hangers on a low rack or hooked over wall pegs.

—A regular miniature doll house and Mommy and Daddy, Sister and Brother dolls will generate play about home life.

—A housekeeping corner in the playroom can be outfitted with child-sized kitchen furniture, such as a sink, stove, cabinet, chest of drawers, table and chairs, spoonware, plastic play foods, metal dishes, utensils, napkins, etc. Paper plates and disposable plastic spoonware are easier to maintain than metalware and the children can drink water or eat real food without adults having to first thoroughly wash all the dishes. Also useful in the home corner are a full-length mirror, toy ironing board and iron.

–Small dolls, large dolls, washable, stuffed with nylon or Dacron representing various family members and medical staff, to be cared for, played with, given "real" shots and bathed. Doll play can allow the child the chance to imagine that he is strong and better able to protect himself and by playing the part of "mommy" the child can reinforce her reality even though they are separated from each other.

Storytelling

Almost every hospital has a library of children's books, which should be freely used, kept unlocked and available at all times. A softly read story can be very comforting to a sick child.

Group story telling or reading can promote discussion on such topics as going to the hospital, spending the night away from home, nightmares and scarey things, doctor's tools, family members and punishment. Children often enjoy storytelling themselves and the use of a tape recorder at these times may prove enlightening to staff, students or volunteers who missed hearing the original. Tape recorders also promote children to tell stories "so that others may hear."

Making a book about the hospital is another way for the child to express feelings and it reveals to parents and staff some of the concerns of the child. He may draw pictures or cut them out of magazines. One four-year-old included in hers a magazine picture of her "doctor when he was a little boy," a real band-aid that covered a drawing of her stitches, a greeting card picture of the "funny bathtub in the hospital," a magazine picture of the playlady and a "real tongue depressor like the one they used on me." Besides the satisfaction she got from making her own book, she was invited to show it and tell her story to other children in the playroom. After discharge, her mother said, she referred to it many times.

Publishing a Newspaper

Some therapeutic play programs value storytelling and written expression so much that they publish a regular pediatric newspaper. It provides the child a chance to talk with a "reporter" or write about some of the things that are different from his everyday life or that irk him. For example, a twelve-year-old wrote:

> The Bathrooms Bug Me!
>
> There is one thing that bugs me, the bathrooms! Because if you have to go to the bathroom and someone locked the door from the other side, you've got a problem and I've locked the other door, once they locked it on me! Why can't they have one bathroom per room? That would keep you out of trouble.

Being sick, with so much being done to you and for you in a hospital, patients can often take on a very passive role. This is counter-balanced somewhat by "reporting" for the pediatric paper. A newspaper can encourage activity by involving children in writing, drawing, typing, reporting, stapling and distributing newspapers. It also encourages an active role in voicing one's feelings. A thirteen-year-old, upset by the lessening of control of her limbs from arthritis, answered the reporter's question "What do doctors do?" by saying, "they poke people, that's all they've been doing to me – jabbing me, and they ask a bunch of dumb questions."

Sometimes writing helps a child to feel more in control, thus lessening the fear that he is at the mercy of staff members. When asked how she would run the hospital, a fifteen-year-old replied that she would "fire everyone and let the kids run the hospital."

Children often write about or draw something that they will not bring up in conversation. When an eleven-year-old who has been hospitalized many times for plastic surgery was asked to draw a picture of things he saw in the hospital, he drew a boy being wheeled on a guerney to the operating room. On the door to the room he drew a large "No Admittance" sign.

So much goes on in a hospital that can tear down a child's image of himself. Procedures that seem too difficult to cope with, body changes that occur as a result of illness or medications, people doing things for you that you used to do yourself, loss of

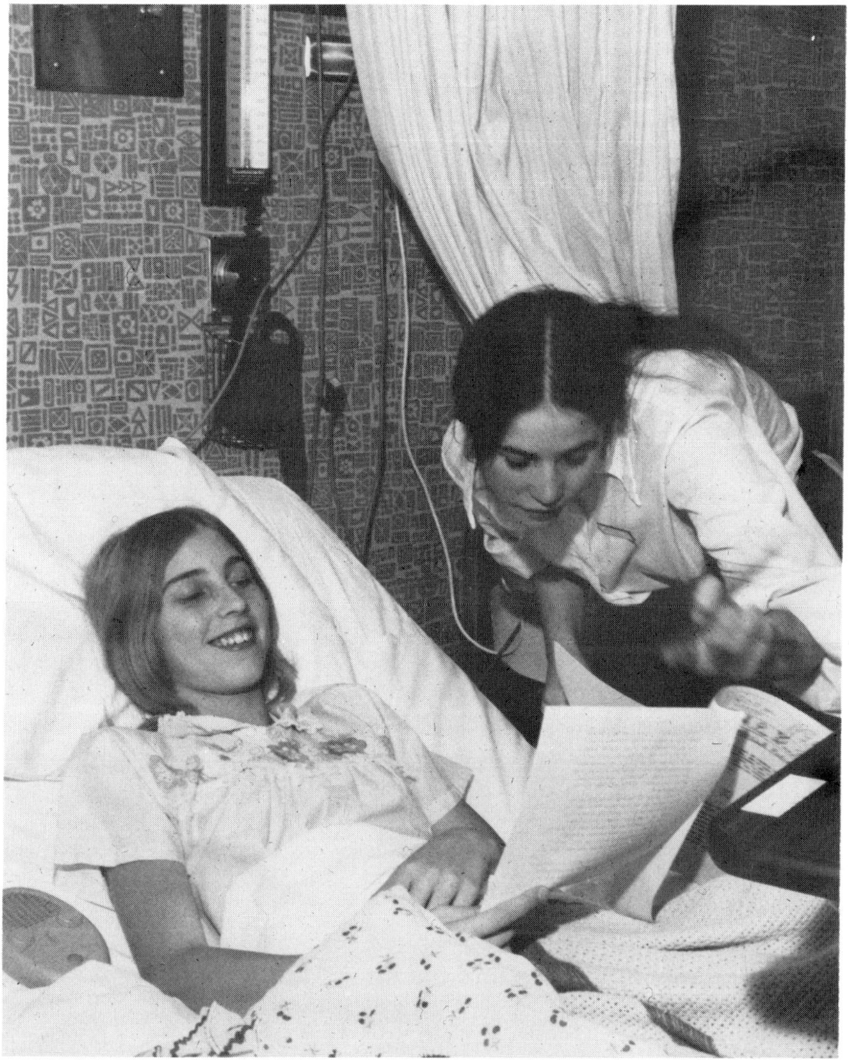

Figure 1 – Contributing to the hospital newspaper provides the pediatric patient with a chance to talk about some of the things she is experiencing that are different from her everyday life.

previously attained developmental plateaus: these are the result of an unfamiliar environment or of the illness itself. All can make a child feel less sure of himself.

The newspaper gives children pride and a sense of accomplishment. Its good effects should not be underestimated.

One child with a low self-image because of the crippling nature of her illness saw her story about receiving an award at school printed on the front page of the hospital paper. The recognition helped her to feel genuinely worthwhile.

Working on a newspaper encourages children to talk about things that have meaning in their everyday life. One adolescent wrote this revealing paragraph about her family:

> I have a pretty good family. But I only have one dumb sister. She is older than me. She also forgets a lot. I wish I had a brother to beat her up. My parents are very pretty and smart, just like me. And last but not least is my dog. She is very good, too. She is bad once in a while. (But not like my sister!)

Children could write about events going on in the hospital that ordinarily happen at home. A child-authored story about Halloween Trick-or-Treating in the hospital might help a new patient realize that people care about what is important to him and that a hospital is not so foreign after all.

Whether child or adult, we all feel comforted when facing unpleasant situations if we know that others share our feelings. Since many children use the newspaper to express gripes or worries, it is easy and comforting for a youthful reader to find an expression of some of his own feelings. A fourteen-year-old boy wrote, "If the doctors don't operate on me pretty soon, I'm going to kill them," expressing an opinion common to hospitalized people tired of all the tests and the uncertainty of what is to come.

Through written media, a child can also tell another patient what something will be like. All the reassurance in the world from an adult may not do as much good as a few words from another child who has already "had it done." A ten-year-old boy expressed it this way:

> When I came to the hospital, I felt fine. Then after two days of being in the hospital, I felt terrible. Now after four days, I feel like a new person, so if you are scared, don't worry, the hospital is the best place in the world to be. So don't be scared no more. You're in good hands.

A ward newspaper offers continuity for chronic pediatric patients who will need recurrent hospitalizations. Since hospitalization plays a major role in their lives, it is important to provide a positive link to that experience. Patients look forward to receiving papers after discharge to hear about their "home away from home." Many patients continue to send stories and pictures after they have been discharged. On their return patients are very pleased to see some of their old contributions posted on bulletin boards. One such instance occurred with a fifteen-year-old boy who was hospitalized again and found in the files an issue from three years back when he was sending valentines to the girl across the hall. He laughed as he shared it with family and staff.

A newspaper is useful to parents as well. It offers a chance for a mother to write while her bed-rest child dictates a story. Or, a parent can write the comments of her very young child. Many are as proud as their children when they see their child's work in print and they want copies for all their relatives. It also helps a parent to understand some of the things his child may be feeling but does not want to talk about.

A child's newspaper can likewise be beneficial to staff because it could give them insights into their patient's reactions to hospitalization. When asked "What is a hospital?", a quiet thirteen-year-old said, "A great big shot needle." Three older patients, writing about ways they would change the hospital said that they would prefer more doctors like the one who "let me cut and take out my own catheter and the ones who let me wrap my own bandages — not like those guys at the doctor's office, they just rip it off when they come to a sore. They don't care if it hurts or not!" A sixteen-year-old stated one of her three wishes was hoping that her scar would not show when she wore her bikini.

The staff can gain a feeling about what children are like at different age levels if ages follow each person's name. A fifteen-year-old girl made an impact on the staff when they read the "Dear Hospital Hannah" column she authored:

Dear Hospital Hannah,
What do I do about a boy who won't grow up?
Mom

Dear Mom,
Give him some room and let him go.
Hospital Hannah, 15 years old

The paper is useful to staff in another very important way. When children write stories or draw pictures of favorite doctors or nurses or when they gripe about the way they have been treated, those persons are sure to hear about it. In either case, patients' likes and dislikes are expressed and sensitive staff may decide to change behavior accordingly.

The administrative personnel who read the children's paper, for example, might be quite enlightened by some of the children's comments. After they read about how a four-year-old hates being in the hospital "because mommy can't stay at night-time," or "they took my mommy away," they might reconsider restrictive policies against rooming-in for parents.

The list of sound reasons for having a paper could be stated indefinitely, but it is important to find out how to do it.

Suggestions for Beginning a Newspaper

1. Select a name by asking for ideas from patients, parents, volunteers and staff.
2. Select an easily accessible location such as a drawer or a box for patients to place their contributions.
3. Have pencils, paper and previous issues nearby.
4. Make up a notebook of interview questions for the first issue that can be used by a volunteer with a patient or by an older patient with a younger patient during an initial meeting. Write these questions — one to a page or one to every other page — so that all answers are in the same place for later typing. The questions might be worded in such a way that they would encourage a child to talk about himself, how he feels about and understands the hospital, and something about particular holi-

days or seasons and what they mean to the child in the hospital.

5. Decide how often it is desirable or possible to publish a paper. Is there enough interest in the project and help to do it once a week or only once a month?
6. Talk with volunteers or staff about methods of approaching and talking with children and for stimulating interest in the paper.
7. If there are no available secretarial services, find a volunteer who would be willing to type the paper and perhaps do the layout. Adolescent patients often enjoy and are good at helping with this.
8. Decide what method will be used for making copies of the paper. A photostencil or Xerox machine allows for flexibility in the original. Stories can be typed when the help is available, then they can be cut out and taped to a blank sheet of paper along with pictures children have drawn. Although colored paper can be used, there is no way to produce colored pictures with this method. Colored ink is possible with a mimeographer, but it means pictures must be drawn on a master. Although the methods for copying will depend on what is available and easiest to manage, it is important to learn in advance about such things as necessary margins and the type of ink that will duplicate best.
9. If the duplicating process chosen is done by a special department in your hospital, meet the people who work there. Let them know how often to expect your order and who will deliver it. They can give suggestions about the best ways to do the printing.
10. Select a file cabinet or drawer to store the following: a) original copies of each newspaper, b) stencils or masters of each issue, c) copies of all newspapers filed chronologically to give on request, d) an up-to-date mailing list, e) extra stories or pictures for future issues and f) newspaper headings for future issues if you have one child who can make a number of them ahead of time.
11. Begin a distribution list. Not only patients, but doctors,

nurses and administrators should receive copies since the paper often contains expressions of patients' true feelings about hospitalization and illness. Include supporting groups on the mailing list; besides writing "thank you" notes to them for their philanthropic contributions, thank them publicly in the newspaper. Hospital departments such as carpentry, house-cleaning and maintenance should also be on the list because they often like to post the paper on their bulletin boards.

12. To publicize the work even more widely, put up a bulletin board about the newspaper. Whenever a new issue comes out, be sure to give copies to current patients, leaving some for parents and staff.

Sensory Experiences

Encourage children to express their ideas and reactions not only through verbal, pictorial or graphic means, but also through kinesthetic and other sensory means. For example, children like:

—Feeling — insert various familiar items into a closed box through a hole in its side, then let a child put a hand in and guess what the items are.

—Smelling — an alcohol swab, soap, vanilla extract, cinnamon

—Tasting — sugar, lemon, salt, onion

Messy Play

So-called "messy play" lures a child into relaxing, nondemanding, expressive play, that allows him to take any direction he chooses. In a group situation, children meet each other and share playful exchanges. Types of "messy play" enjoyed by children and possible in a supervised play program are:

—Play dough or clay: This is most enjoyed when the children make it themselves from equal parts of flour and salt with ¼ part water and ¼ part vegetable shortening added until the consistency of clay is reached; to brighten it with color, use water that has tempera powder paint or food coloring mixed in.

—Fingerpaint, shaving cream or soap foams: Aerosol shaving cream can be squirted right on the table. Tempera paint

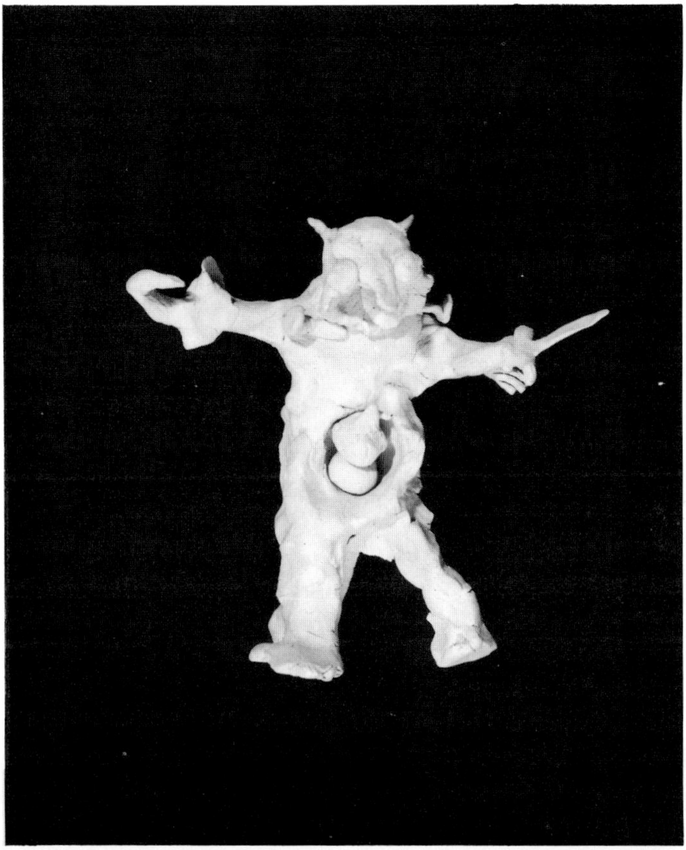

Figure 2 – A clay person created by a pediatric urology patient. "This doctor has acupuncture through the neck, a swollen bladder, one kidney, a hook arm and a sterile switchblade."

can also be added. When there is a longer period of time for the activity, the children can use eggbeaters to make a shaving cream kind of consistency from three parts soap flakes and one part water. Older children can help the young ones with the beating.

–Sand, sawdust or cornmeal: If there is no outside area and playroom space is ample, buy or create a sand table with a lid. (It can do double duty as a table part of the time.) Sand can also be put into dishpans or plastic lined boxes so a child can play with it in bed. Be sure an extra sheet or covering protects the child. Funnels, sifters, containers, spoons, plastic people, cars and small blocks all add to the enjoyment of sand-box play.

—Cornstarch mixture: Mix one box of cornstarch and one cup water to make a "magic" mixture that is sometimes liquid and sometimes solid.

—Sticky glue: Let the children make it themselves from flour and water.

—Water play: Children LOVE to play in water. It is *the* most universally popular "messy" medium wherever it is contained: in a large photo developing tray, small bowl, sink or bathtub, indoors or out. Water relaxes children and can have a rich variety of "props" to use in play such as: intravenous tubing and syringes, funnels, cups, sponges, boats and plastic toys. Outside, give them paint brushes and a can of water or a sprinkling can, and add soap or coloring to the tub of water to double the fun. Children can wash things for hours and be happy. They enjoy washing dolls, doll clothes, toy dishes, doll house furniture, all toys, themselves and their own clothes.

—Bubble blowing: Buy the commercial solution in a plastic bottle or make your own solution from liquid detergent and water. The "bubble ring" comes with the commercial variety and a "do-it-yourself" bubble ring can be a pair of dime-store glasses with the lenses removed. (This not only provides fun but is also therapeutic for the child who needs breathing exercises.)

Play that is "messy" is not necessarily dirty, wild, loud or uncontrolled. It must have limits as should all play. These limits will require that the children have some control over the situation, so that while they can still feel free to explore the "messy media" uninhibitedly, they will be unafraid of accidents that could cause them discomfort or a scolding.

It is helpful for the play director to insist on:

—The use of slip-on plastic aprons, made from a single piece of plastic, with Velcro closure.

—Defined containers such as tubs for water, large table or photo developing tray for finger paint, and dishpans or cafeteria trays for cornmeal.

—A protected surface upon which to work such as a washable tabletop for shaving cream painting, a sheet under the water-play tubs, a plastic sheet under a towel for a bed patient who wants to blow bubbles, and wood boards or oilcloth upon which to work in clay.

—Carefully selected items for water-play such as funnels, strainers, plastic containers, measuring cups, medicine droppers, syringes and ear bulbs, but *not* wood blocks that will warp or bean bags that will split or glass that will break.

Active Play

Most children are not used to being inside and quiet all of the time. Even in a hospital they need chances to move and be active. They need time to punch, tear, throw and wrestle as outlets for the strong feelings they have about being sick, having painful things done to them and being away from their families. As much of this should be allowed as the doctor's orders permit. However, supervision is important during such activities as these physical activities could promote over-excitement.

Here are examples of active play that have been used successfully both indoors and outside in a medical setting. Some are necessarily noisy and some are quiet. Do not expect a child to beat a drum "quietly." Rather, give him a pillow to do so if quiet must be observed.

—Throwing: sponge balls, ring toss, frisbees, balloons, bean bags, soft rubber balls and "basketball" (a hoop basket can be made from a wire coathanger bent over a door. For a child in traction a sponge ball could be threaded with string or ribbon so the child can retrieve it himself).

—Hammering: nails in wood, commercial pounding benches, pegs into clay.

—Beating: drum, pillows, stuffed toy.

—Punching: balloons (suspended on a string from ceiling, door frame, or traction bar), sponge balls, or punching bags (can be hand made from a 2-layered bag stuffed with beans or sawdust).

—Jumping: hopscotch (installed with different colored tile on floor, or painted or taped on), jump rope.

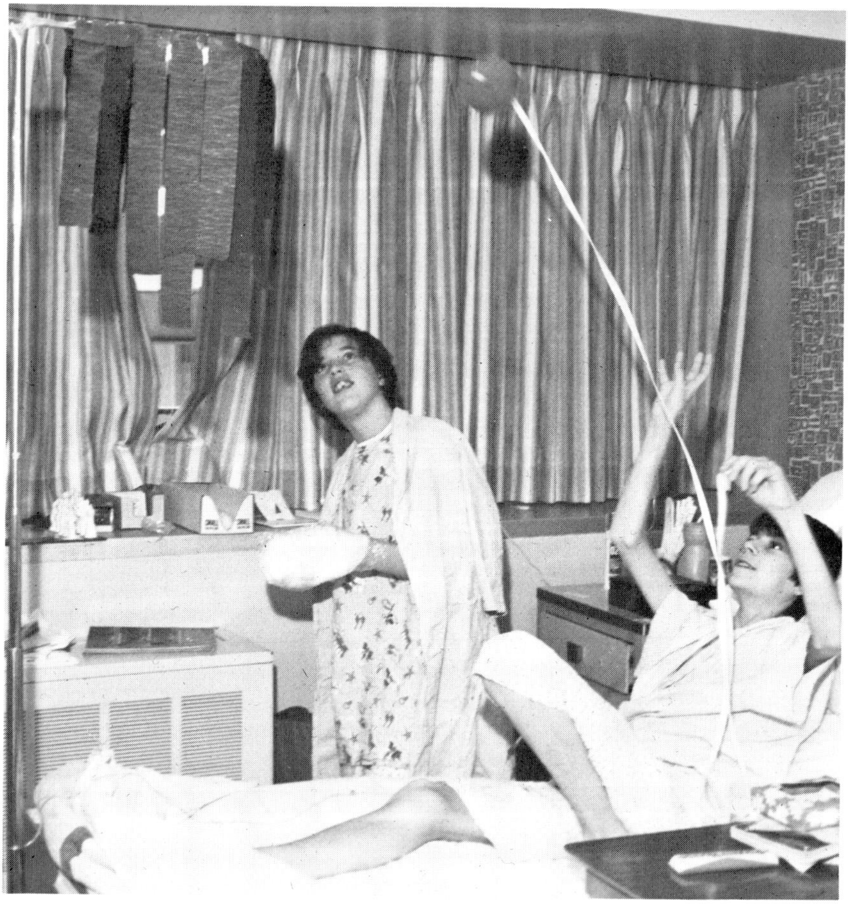

Figure 3 — A sponge "basketball" attached to a retrieval cord and a hoop made of a coathanger provide therapeutic play for a bedrest patient and his friend.

—Tearing: paper, clay, play dough.
—Riding: tricycle, plastic cars, wheelchairs, guerneys.
—Wrestling: big stuffed animal, bean-bag chair, beach ball.
—Marching: to the beat of a drum, tambourine, harmonica or stamping of feet.
—Dancing: to music of radio, phonograph, or singing and humming (with scarves or crepe paper streamers).
—Pushing: wheelchairs, baby buggy, tricycles, guerneys, plastic cars, big plastic balls.

Art

Since children who come to a medical facility are under certain tensions to begin with, it is unwise to add more stress by giving them exacting commercial pictures to color in neat shapes, to cut perfectly or to trace. Although some children might want this kind of rigid work and even gain some security in their ability to do it, most do not thrive under this added pressure.

Therefore, drawing, painting or other visual forms of artistic or asthetic construction should be left to the child's imagination and need. This includes such activities as decorations, design work, creating doll clothes, making posters and signs, illustrating, and using paper of various sizes, shapes and colors; using chalk, crayons, watercolors, brushes, oils, tempera, fluorescents, felt pens, clay sculpture, plaster of paris and papier-mache.

It also means unstructured freedom in photography. Ask a child to photograph a story of what it is like to come to the hospital. The eight-year-old is likely to snap the playroom and the toys. The adolescent is more likely to photograph his room and roommates, the staff, gadgets and medicines. Using Poloroid film the child gets instant feedback and sees himself in a new perspective. If he saves a first-day photo and compares it to a discharge-day photo, he will see for himself the progress he has made. Clinic children who take each other's pictures regularly see themselves as they grow taller and more mature at each visit.

Art work is also a very helpful tool for the play director to use in getting to know the children as individuals. The way one child uses the media and the work he produces reveals that particular child in an expressive way that might take hours of conversation to duplicate.

Crafts

"Making something" not only occupies a child's time, it can also provide the companionship of the group and an outlet for tension. When children are grouped around a table or sit on the floor or a sheet or rug and their apparent focus is on the object being created, they feel safe to talk to each other at random. Among the topics sure to be raised is their medical experience. An effective group leader facilitates this discussion, while ensuring that the supplies that are needed are there so that the activity, flowing smoothly, does not interrupt the communication.

Crafts, then, is a vehicle to reach children, not an end in itself. The goal is not only to put together a product but to provide a familiar setting in which a child can feel comfortable and safe. For this reason, do not encourage the use of contests, comparisons, prizes or races to finish quickly.

A craft will vary with the various ages of children who will work at it and should be selected to be suitable to their needs. For example: In "making a belt" out of leather loops, the younger child may simply carry a loop with him, feeling the quality of the fabric, comparing the rough to the smooth side, fitting a finger through the hole. The older child may attempt to attach the pieces together. The adolescent will easily make the belt and may make creative improvements. Even when there is a separate area for "adolescents" or "toddlers" there will be variations in the group that should be recognized.

Start a program by ordering a minimum of high cost commercial items and use "scrapcrafting" instead. Materials for scrapcrafting are ingenious, not expensive. Some suggestions:

—Puzzles: Paste colorful magazine picture on cardboard. Cut into pieces. Store in an envelope.

—Clock: Attach brad fastener in center of paper plate. Write in clock numbers. Use to indicate when next medication comes, or mealtime, or visitors, or bedtime.

—Walking doll: Poke two holes near top of paper cup. Turn cup upside down. Put two fingers into holes from inside of cup to outside and walk them. For more detail, draw features on cup.

—Treasure pull: Tie a string on one side of shoebox. Tightly tie a large bead or other easily-held, but not easily-swallowed object on end of string. Child can put any treasure doll or book or other item to carry into the box.

—Spring basket: Decorate plastic strawberry baskets with colored crepe paper, cotton buds, fabric scraps and foil.

—"What is it?": Start with a base. It could be a cardboard, a piece of wood, styrofoam or the reverse side of the wood backing of a puzzle whose pieces are lost. Add objects to it with paste to make it high and wide. Try wood scraps, popsicle stick, tongue blades, plastic pieces lost from games, cards from an incomplete deck. If mostly wood, it can be painted.

—Beads: Dye plastic I.V. tubing and cut for stringing on telephone wire. Straws and styrofoam packing material are also fun for the young child to string.

Parents benefit from working on a craft activity alongside their child or while waiting for their child to return from a test, as it relaxes them. Some offer craft ideas and bring in scrap materials. Making something for their child while he is occupied with medical procedures can help to ease a parent's helpless feeling. The more familiar the craft is to parents the more likely they are to repeat the activity at home for the patient and for his siblings and friends.

Games

Games are fun and also therapeutic – there is such a variety in the world of games that they answer many needs. For instance:

—A shy or withdrawn child can get to know and trust a staff person through the one-to-one contact of a game.

—Parents and children can use familiar games as a means of passing time and keeping a link with home.

—Patients will get to know each other, talk informally and share common concerns while playing.

—Children with limited activity may be helped by being able to move the parts of a game.

—A staff person or volunteer spending time with a particular child may find a game an easy way to "break the ice."

—Many adults find that a board game is more familiar to them and, therefore, more comfortable than other types of play.

—Because games are usually self-contained in an easily storable and transportable box they may be one activity that can be used by children after the play program is closed for the day.

—Group games such as musical chairs (or musical hats if activity is restricted) can be used to help children get to know each other and as a boisterous way to use pent-up energy.

Building and Manipulation

Building and manipulative materials offer the hospitalized child a chance to exercise his dexterity, ingenuity, problem-solving ability and strength. Dependent in the hospital upon people other than his parents and confronted with the unfamiliar, he profits by this chance to be in control and to manipulate.

Suggestions for materials:

–A low workbench with vises would be helpful as tools, as well as hammers, saws, a drill, a rasp, a file, screw drivers, wrench, assorted large nails and screws, clamps and sandpaper. Accessories also motivate! Try providing the young builder with washers, plumbing parts, wire, nuts and bolts, hooks and eyes.

–The commercial sets that have many pieces that can be arranged into buildings, designs or boxes. These include: Lincoln Logs, Lego, Tinker Toys, Erector set, Crystal Climbers, Stacking Clowns, Plastic Snowflakes and various sizes of blocks.

–The commercial manipulative boards, such as Busy Box, Mesh Gears, Lock Box. Homemade versions of these, using hardware, gears, plumbing, jar lids and fasteners can be simply made. A wood plaque the length of the examining table can be attached to the wall above the table with circles to turn, doors to open, and figures to move. These devices are also useful in unsupervised waiting rooms, where building sets with small pieces would soon be lost.

–The commercial manipulative items that encourage use of fine motor skills and help the child to have feelings of mastery with successful use. These include such items as a sorting box, graduated stack of rings, puzzles, parquetry blocks, stringing beads and metal frames with fit-in shapes.

–The large construction work done by children from found materials: turning cartons into a house, a castle, a fire station or a space capsule depending on how a particular group of children cut it and decorate it; using scrap lumber to build a structure large and sturdy enough to climb into; stretching sheets or fabric over a slide or large table to create a house inside.

—The sturdy, longer-lasting objects made by children that they can take home; musical instruments, wood sculpture from glued or nailed wood leftovers, scrapbooks from Christmas card catalogs.

Special Events

For some children staying long enough, the hospital becomes a second home, but an emergency patient with no preparation for coming to the hospital may feel quite disoriented. Even the first day out of his room, such a patient should be helped to understand where he is in relation to places on the ward that are familiar to him or that he will need to contact, i.e. kitchen, play area or adolescent recreation room, bath and shower area, parents' waiting room. When he is well enough, he might want to visit other parts of the hospital.

Trips around the hospital also help to fight boredom. A child looks forward to going to such places as carpentry, the gift shop or the library, and talking about it before, during and after the trip.

Something special should always be planned for birthdays and holidays although parties and entertainment should not be overemphasized. Halloween can be a treat for the whole hospital if children are taken trick-or-treating to the various departments that they have visited for medical care, to scare them in return.

Once a play program is established it will become the screening ground for all visitors who want to entertain or plan a party for the children. Be ready to say "No" if it is already too busy at Christmas or if it sounds like the magic tricks may be a little too scary. Many times, though, offers can be welcomed. Keep a file to remember the regular favorites.

Medical Information

Children's natural curiosity, as well as their desire for information in order to make sense out of the confusion of illness, creates a motivation to learn about the hospital facility, the staff and themselves. Although some children take indirect avenues to explore medical instrumentation and roles, others want direct answers to their questions. Sometimes, however, these children need help in forming the questions they want to ask because they lack knowledge about themselves and their illness.

It is helpful to have various doctors, nurses, physical therapists and other "hands-on" personnel visit with the children to answer questions, demonstrate machinery and reassure young patients.

In one successful orthopedic clinic, a doctor spends thirty minutes in the playroom waiting room putting casts on large dolls, while children help and ask questions. Then, the play director encourages the children to react through pictures and stories. Later the doctor returns and cuts off the doll's dry cast with a noisy cast-cutter, explaining the machine and letting the children imitate the sound of the saw. When the doll is "well," they realize that only the cast is cut, not the limb. This doctor is wise in the ways of children and knows they profit more from a real experience than from verbal descriptions.

Another similar minded doctor brings venipuncture supplies to explain blood drawings to the children and, with the help of a reluctantly willing intern, to demonstrate the procedure. Many of them had experienced it but few had seen it done, because they are usually told to look away. Fewer still knew why it had to be done or what information could be "read" in their blood. The matter-of-fact objectivity of this approach dispelled at least some of the children's apprehension about a common – but alarming – hospital procedure.

The EKG can be demonstrated with a doll. One successful cardiologist with a special understanding of children's silent fears wheels the portable electrocardiogram machine to the hospital playroom and attaches the electrodes to a life-size doll. The children see that the electrodes do not penetrate the skin and learn that the doctor cannot tell what you ate or know what you are thinking when he uses the EKG. Then, the children built a toy EKG from a box and painted dials on it, outfitted it with discarded EKG tapes and finally reenacted the EKG "drama" delightedly and repeatedly.

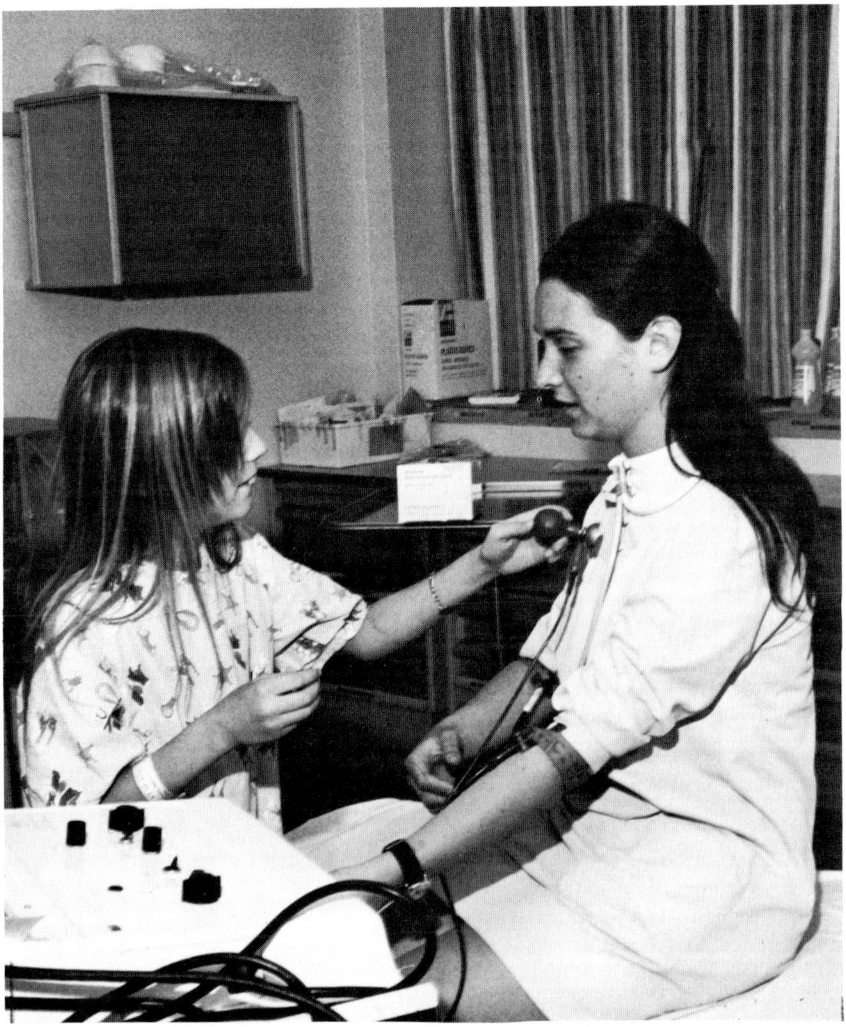

Figure 4 — This child not only explores the equipment, but she also repeats a recent experience with the nurse.

This machinery should be shown to children even when it will not be used on all of them because children see it used on other patients, perhaps a roommate and wonder not only what it is but will it be used on them. Simple reassurance during these sessions has obvious benefits in diminishing their concerns.

Other ways that children can learn what they want to know

is to go on *tours of certain parts of the hospital or the unit.* This allays fantasy fears and substitutes reality. For example, a ten-year old child on bedrest who sees equipment rushed into a room on the next corridor, may fantasize about the episode. To relieve his confusion, his entire bed can be wheeled to that corridor where reality will probably prove less frightening than his fantasy. Going on such a "tour" serves double duty for it also reassures him that he is not critically ill, although he may be confined to bed.

Older children could be asked to orient new patients and it is a good time for the play director to listen to check on the accuracy of information. If the treatment room is referred to as the torture chamber, it will be necessary to intervene for the veteran as well as for the rookie.

In the waiting room of the outpatient clinic, or on the ward, regular and consistent informal meetings of the play director with parents and children are a *must* to clarify or answer nonmedical questions and to encourage parents to let the doctor know of any special concerns.

Normal Living Experiences

When one is ill or injured and then separated from normal living patterns, there is an added strain of discomfort. It is most acute with the pediatric patient. Nothing will make a hospital as relaxed as home, but there are some simple steps that a play director can take to introduce a semblance of familiarity into a hospital's foreign routine, and thereby, to make patients happier and more secure. Against the unfamiliarity and loneliness of the hospital setting, a play program offers various activities that are consistent with a child's normal living pattern. For instance:

- —Family-type interaction: older children can help younger ones in the playroom.
- —Normal jobs and duties: children could help in cleaning and setting up the playroom.
- —Adolescent grooming: cosmetic supplies should be available for older girls to borrow for hair dressing and make-up experimentation.
- —Parent-child "sharing": older children and parents could help to mend broken toys and make miniaturizations of equipment.

—Imitative learning: young children might "help" the housekeeping staff as they clean and straighten the bedroom and playroom.

—School: missing school can be upsetting to some children. They worry that they will fall behind or even be put back a grade. While some children are not worried about it initially, their parents are, and that worry is transmitted to the child. Many Boards of Education provide hospital school teachers, but if the hospital is not that fortunate, then think about setting up a school through the play program. Many hours of the school age child's life can be constructively absorbed in educational play. Besides a normal routine, school offers some children a feeling of confidence that the staff and his parents believe he is getting better.

—Meals: eating on a tray in bed is unusual for most children and reinforces the dependent, sick role. A shared meal can promote normalcy and encourages social interchanges. It counteracts the loneliness that eating alone in bed invites. At a shared meal, one staff person — a nurse, a play staffer — can supervise and also take note of the social dynamics. Grouping also provides a setting for discussion of good nutrition, meal patterns at home and favorite foods. Providing a family style meal where each food is brought in a dish and served at the table further enhances this idea. The child serves himself the portions he thinks he can eat. It is a real feeling of accomplishment when he can go back for seconds. If he is not feeling well enough to do this, the parent can serve him his food just as at home. A great deal can be noted about the parent-child relationship during such a setting. The playroom is a good setting for meals, but a separate dining area would be better.

—Food preparation: although the very young child is not always given the opportunity to prepare his own snacks at home, the experience is generally familiar. To do the same thing in the playroom (or at bedside for a nonambulatory patient) can be very satisfying to the hospitalized child on a regular diet. While the snack is cooking or baking, the children could clean up their work space and then create poems, stories or songs about what they have been doing. Many healthy snacks are so-called "finger foods," such as: carrots, celery, cucumber, cherry or plum tomatoes, zucchini, turnip, lettuce, peaches, apples, bananas, melons, oranges, apricots, prunes and plums.

Sweet starchy things are sometimes fun to make such as: cake and cookie mixes, refrigerator Slice-and-Bake cookies, cakes "from scratch," fruit loaves such as banana or applesauce loaf and frosting for ready-made cookies. Familiar favorites include hot dogs, crackers, peanut butter and jelly sandwiches, bologna and cheese, bacon lettuce and tomato, jello (can be made in medicine cups), fruit juice, punch and popcorn.

The food can then be distributed by the children in small portions to themselves, their families and the staff. This is usually well received because when a child has a chance to distribute a product he has created he is giving something of himself. This is particularly meaningful in a pediatric setting where children ordinarily are dependent on what others have to give them, where patients must usually be passive and accept the intrusive actions of helpful adults. In food preparation and serving, however, he can be the boss. He can make his own selections and be in control of results. It also gives the "cooks" a chance to talk about many subjects not necessarily related to food. Those children who cannot directly express their strong feelings about necessary medical experiences may do so indirectly with cutting, peeling, sectioning, curling, mixing, beating and stirring. These experiences are not infrequently the precursor to more direct discussion of their self-concern later.

It is also a means of providing a mid-morning snack to children and families in the clinic, who often sorely need it. In addition, it:

—introduces children to new foods.

—provides samples of snacks that are wholesome, nourishing and inexpensive.

—encourages children to explore the size, shape, texture, length, width, taste and smell of foods.

–promotes the safe and supervised use of peelers and knives, thereby encouraging parents to teach the correct use of kitchen tools. (Childhood accidents seen in emergency rooms are not uncommonly the result of the child's natural curiosity and unsupervised exploration of kitchen supplies, cleaners and equipment.)

–teaches clean food handling, thoughtful set-up and responsible clean-up.

Picnic

Not much in a hospital is fun, but a picnic provides an opportunity for children to have a meal in an enjoyable manner. A barbeque works nicely for serving food such as hot dogs and hamburgers. However, children also enjoy making their own sandwiches from cold cuts or salads, provided by dietary.

Most hospitals have some outdoor area where children, their families and staff can meet for this purpose – weather permitting. In a hospital where siblings are restricted from visiting the wards the picnic provides an opportunity for the well and the hospitalized children to visit together.

Many children respond positively just to getting away from the ward and being in fresh air. Add to this some opportunities for active play, a group song fest with a volunteer guitar player, a chance to share a meal and visit with family members or perhaps to share a lunch with one's doctor or nurse. The picnic proves to be well worth the staff effort involved in carrying it out. Staff who have attended comment that they learn a great deal about their patients and child behavior in general from this informal contact.

It also proves to be a good opportunity to help define the role of the play program with new or uninformed staff because in order to carry out a picnic one needs to know:

–What kind of cooperation will be needed with the ward staff?

–Who will decide which children can attend, what diet they should have and how the substitution will be made for picnic food in place of a tray?

Figure 5 – A picnic is a welcome relief to the constant demands made on pediatric patients.

–Should a meeting be called to discuss these arrangements?
–Will dietary be able to help with possible charges for food of nonpatients? Where will such money be kept and who will manage it?
–Is there enough volunteer or staff help? What kinds of jobs are needed in order to carry out a smooth functioning picnic?

More specifically, make a list of jobs required for the picnic and let volunteers choose how they wish to help, such as the following:

1. Check with nurses to see who can go to picnic.
2. Call dietician to give names of picnicers and arrange for special diets.
3. Talk with children about the event and invite them.

4. Write children's names and note special diets on intake sheet.
5. Get linen, cups, straws, ice, outdoor toys, trash bag, etc., to go to picnic.
6. Pick up food from dietary.
7. Set up barbeque and food outside.
8. Get needed wheelchairs and guerneys.
9. Encourage staff to come.
10. Wait with children at elevator or other exits of the unit.
11. Transport patients to picnic and back.
12. Arrange food and utensils.
13. Cook food.
14. Help children get their lunch.
15. Record children's intake on intake sheet.
16. Return unopened picnic supplies to dietary or ward.
17. Clean picnic grounds.
18. Take picnic lunches to children in ward who could not attend.

One of the reasons that spontaneity and duplication of familiar pleasures is absent from many hospitals is that activities such as preparing snacks or having a picnic requires organization, time, energy and personnel. Although some hospital administrators regard such expenditures as an unjustifiable, indulgent and "faddish" waste, others have come to the realization that a patient's happiness and psychological sense of well-being often do have a direct therapeutic affect on his recovery. They see these activities of the play program as building blocks of recovery.

Music and Sounds

"Quiet please – hospital zone" is a common sign in front of hospitals. Once inside a hospital, is it always quiet? Few wards are as quiet as they are usually thought to be. Listen, for example, to the sounds of television, staff and visitors, floor-clacking shoes, conversational bits at the nurses' station or outside of rooms, doctors' rounds held in hallways, service personnel's equipment in motion, paging systems, emergency buzzers and sometimes construction or traffic sounds outside. A pediatric ward in particular is a place where other sounds familiar to the child should be expected. Although sounds must sometimes be channeled to a different area because a child needs to sleep after surgery or is critically ill, generally the staff should expect music, laughter and loud talk. When children are not used to silence they can become alarmed by the persistent quiet, whereas the "normal" types of sounds would be comforting.

Music that children play themselves or sing, march or dance to can also be helpful in relieving tensions. If a child is not able to get out of his bed or wheelchair to do his normal kind of running and active play, beating a drum or shaking a tambourine can still be fun. The child too shy or withdrawn to express himself verbally in the hospital could gradually join a rhythm band or begin to respond to finger plays. An older child threatened by an illness or loss of control may gain recognition and therefore ego strength by showing off his ability to play the guitar, piano or autoharp. He could also join in group singing or a jam session in a casual, permissive atmosphere.

At one hospital, the children in rooms near the playroom always know when the play director opens the doors in the morning: the record player sends inviting sounds through the hallway.

Commercially made rhythm instruments give better percussion and sound, but they can be effectively improvised with:

—Large cans opened at both ends and covered with inner tube or old drum head strung together to make a drum.

—The lid of a metal container, such as a film cannister, nailed to a piece of dowel. Beans or rice put into a container and twisted shut, using rubber cement to glue lid securely.

—Blocks of wood and sandpaper stapled on, to rub together.

—A stretch elastic sewed into a wristlet, with bells sewn on.

—Halves of coconut shells to clap together.

—Bandage cans filled with pebbles, sand beans, macaroni, rice.

—Drums from oatmeal cartons.

Explore sounds in the room by tapping, clapping, stamping, walking and jumping together. Use the stethoscope for children to listen to each other's heart, chest and back sounds and to the sounds of the pet animals. The tuning fork is also fun. In the intensive care unit, answer children's questions about the sounds they hear from the various constant monitoring devices. In isolation use small portable radios as a source of auditory input.

Music, through records, tape or the parents' voice, can be especially soothing at bedtime. Even a few minutes of a lullaby or message-song can help some children relax enough to fall asleep. If the patient's mother can be there to put her own child to sleep, she may need encouragement to carry on as usual with whatever rocking, talking, singing or humming she usually does.

Natural Science

Children's information about animals, plants and other natural sciences is acquired in random fashion and at various times. To acquire knowledge the child needs first-hand experiences with time to explore events, think about them, verbalize them and systematize them. The same process is needed for the child to learn to understand himself, his body and its workings, why he is in a medical setting, what has happened and will be likely to occur to him physically. Organizing his information and the way he thinks about it gives him a confident sense of order.

—Overcoming fear: fear is an important topic in hospitals and to be treated sometimes it must come out in the open. One hospital had an unusual provocateur – dry and cool, not slimy.

> A pet boa constrictor was brought regularly to visit the children! They had been told earlier about the snake so that they would have some idea of what to expect. Children who were particularly afraid at first felt proud as they mastered their fears, touched the snake and found him friendly. Lots of talk about fears and how to manage them, related to the snake, could soon be transferred in follow-up discussions over drawings into talk of fears about other things: the doctor's equipment, surgery, clinic procedures and visiting other sick people.

The play director's role is not to tell children not to be afraid, but to show by calm conversation and interest that it is safe to talk about fear or scary times if you feel like it.

Animal Therapy

A parent wrote to a hospital administrator: "The animals

were the first thing our son showed any interest in after his surgery, and he laughed for the first time as he watched the hamster running."

Animals have natural appeal for every child for they have life, movement, surprise and noise. They are reassuring in a

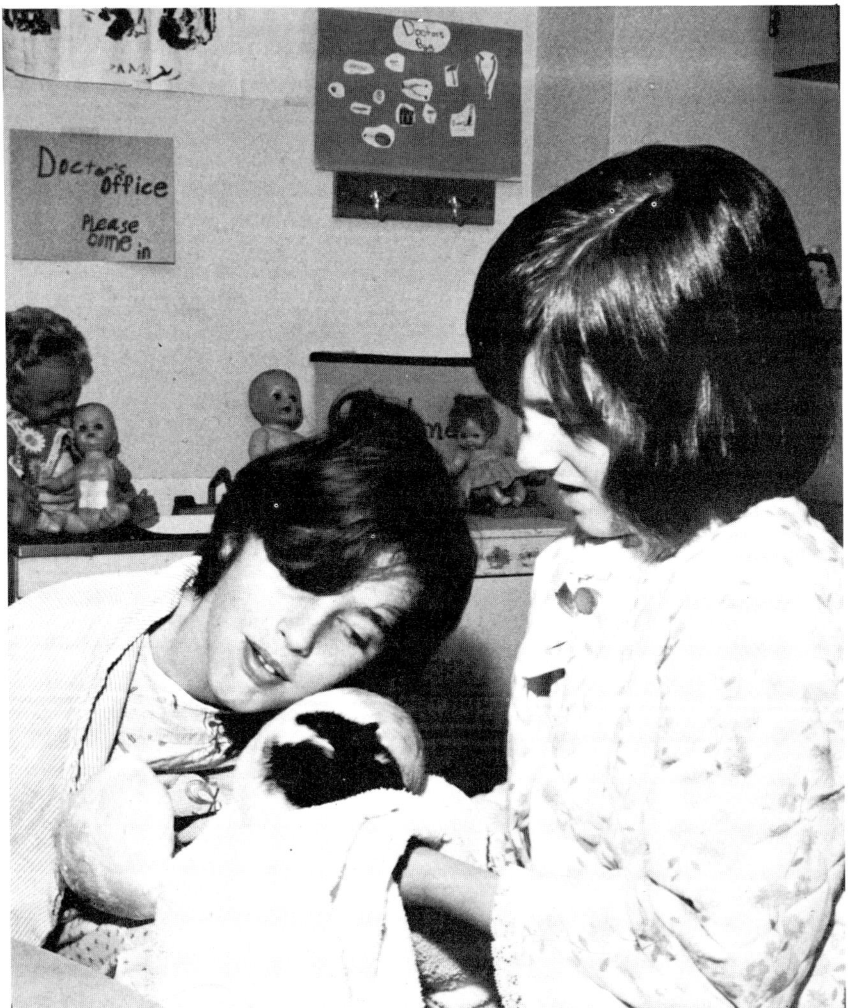

Figure 6 – Animals have natural appeal, as well as being comforting to the sick child.

mechanical environment, nonthreatening, and nothing is required of the child to enjoy them. For nonspeaking children, for those too young to converse and those speaking a language other than English, animals cross the language barrier. They also symbolize a homelike atmosphere. They furnish the basis for conversation about life, birth, death, sibling play, maintaining a home, feeding, nursing, adoption, roles of family members and care of pets. Naturally, there is always the exception to the rules and one should be alert to the possibility of finding a child who is afraid of animals or has been told they are dirty and not to go near them.

CARE OF LIVE ANIMALS. What time and attention should be planned if animals are to be maintained? Which animals should be used? To decide such questions read books on animal care, talk with a veterinarian, a pet show owner, or if the hospital does research with animals, visit the laboratory and speak to the animal handlers there. Care of certain pet animals is simple and routine but obviously must be regular to preserve their health and a clean environment for the children. Check with the Environmental Health Committee in your facility for agreement on how you will care for the animals. Bring along the veterinarian's previously written suggestions or you may have to agree to inordinately elaborate precautions.

When animals except fish are handled regularly, firmly but tenderly and are well fed and cared for they are generally docile and friendly. In case of an animal bite, however, the procedure to follow in the facility should be known.

From time to time children ask to bring their kittens or puppies from home with them to the clinic. Some even want to bring them into the ward. A few hospital authorities do not object as long as the animals are on a leash or in a box or are trained. Others fear fleas or ticks that the animal may bring, allergic reactions to the hair or that a child may be bitten. Mostly they object because of the nuisance and some animals do carry diseases. It is known, for example, that turtles can carry salmonella and birds can carry psitticosis. But clean, well-cared-for animals usually involve no new risk.

A safe easily cleaned cage or other container is a good investment. The wire of the cage should be too small for small fingers to go through. When the animals are being held it helps to have a towel or cloth under them to protect against clawing and messing. Some animals also seem to feel more secure and relax when they are properly supported by a towel.

While some doctors and nurses thoroughly enjoy animals, like to handle them, call them by name and inquire about new breeds, others become upset at even a mention of them! Some medical personnel see the therapeutic value of pets; others regard them as health threats. The same attitudes can be found in parents, so follow their wishes in regard to how closely they want their child to come to any animals.

Presenting the activities suggested in this chapter can be exciting to the worker, the child and his parents. They are good "tools" for helping the child cope with the unfamiliar experience involved in a medical setting. However, that is exactly what they are — tools. Alone they can never substitute for the very essential relationship developed between the child and the helping adult. The child coming to a medical setting may not be healthy, but his entire body may not be affected. He needs a semblance of normal life activity and play, an outlet for his curiosity and continuing informal educational experiences of the widest possible scope and interest.

Chapter 7

ANSWERING QUESTIONS ABOUT A PLAY PROGRAM

The ten most often asked questions about the advisability of setting up, maintaining and funding an in-hospital or clinic play program for children.

ANY NEW PROGRAM in a hospital must justify its goals, initial cost, occupation of space and the policy changes required to implement it. The following are commonly heard when a therapeutic play program is new or needs to grow:

1. "A PLAY PROGRAM IS A GOOD IDEA, BUT IT'S MORE IMPORTANT TO TAKE CARE OF THE CHILD'S PHYSICAL HEALTH. THAT'S WHAT HE COMES TO US FOR. IF WE DON'T CURE HIS BODY IT DOESN'T HELP TO WARM HIS PSYCHE."

It is not an "either-or" situation; of course a medical facility is dedicated to healing bodies. Of course, a "warmed" psyche, like warm chicken soup, is not enough to cure disease and mend bones. But a physical-only approach is only half an approach. The body and the spirit must be cared for simultaneously.

Caring about a child's reactions to imminent pain or to alteration of his body is not only charitable – it is good common sense: we cannot expect a child to be cooperative, optimistic or master the situation without giving him information and reassurance to reduce his tension. Difficult enough for an adult, anxiety is far more of a problem for the young child. He does not understand why he must submit to restrictions, demands and bodily intrusions, and he often feels helpless in the face of an overwhelming experience.

In a therapeutic play program staffed with people trained to help him, the ill child can learn to accept the reasons for his hospitalization, treatment or procedures. His active participation and reduced stress can speed his recovery. Parents find allies in their efforts to give him this emotional support. An environment such as this promotes good mental health.

2. "IT'S A GOOD IDEA, BUT COULDN'T VOLUNTEERS PLAY WITH CHILDREN? WHY DO WE HAVE TO PAY SOMEONE TO DO THAT?"

A successful program calls for a high degree of professionalism, though it may use paraprofessional aid as well.

For example, in supplementing the physical contact and motherly attention which concerned nurses can give to patients, volunteers are essential. Volunteers cannot carry on a therapeutic play program alone, however, because they are not usually trained to observe situations requiring therapeutic interventions, do not have authority, may have emotional involvements with children who are seriously ill or who have died which interfere with their ability to render suitable assistance and they usually are not available enough on a regular basis to provide the consistency and continuity required to have a stable program.

It takes an experienced, trained professional to design a therapeutic play setting, to create a climate of support and to react constructively — not just sympathetically — to frightened, ill or emotionally affected children.

3. "WHY DO WE NEED A PLAYROOM? SPACE IS AT A PREMIUM! CAN'T THE PLAY DIRECTOR BRING A TOY CART AROUND FROM ROOM TO ROOM? OR, CAN'T SHE USE THE CONFERENCE ROOM TWO HOURS A DAY? (UNLESS THE DOCTORS NEED IT, OF COURSE.)"

Hospitalized children need a safe haven from beds, bedrooms, treatment rooms and conference rooms in which they are always available for examination. They need a place to call their own which is secure and familiar. A child in a hospital needs the psychological safety, social interaction and familiar comfort of a playroom. Staff members often state their need for a conference room, staff restroom, writing or interview room, consultation or chart room and lounge or coffee room. The child patient – who is the reason for having a staff – needs a bedroom, a bathroom *and a playroom.*

4. "WHY DO WE NEED A PLAY DIRECTOR? THERE IS A SECRETARY (RECEPTIONIST, INFORMATION DESK CLERK, WARD CLERK, ETC.) IN THE CLINIC WAITING ROOM (OR, JUST OUTSIDE THE WARD PLAYROOM.) SHE GETS TO KNOW THE FAMILIES AND CAN GIVE OBSERVATIONS TO THE DOCTORS. SHE CAN KEEP AN EYE ON TOYS."

A secretary who has full responsibility to her job, does not usually have the time, the background or the interest to make meaningful observations. One cannot combine jobs and expect to have either job done well; neither can one expect a secretary to do a sociologist's or psychologist's work.

5. "A PLAY PROGRAM IS UNNECESSARY–IT WOULD DUPLICATE DUTIES. OUR NURSES ALREADY DO BEHAVIORAL OBSERVATIONS; PARENTS ARE KNOWLEDGEABLE THESE DAYS AND PREPARE THEIR CHILDREN; DOCTORS MAKE EVERY EFFORT NOT TO UNNECESSARILY HURT THEIR PATIENTS; VOLUNTEERS BRING TOYS."

Children's needs are frequently not as fulfilled as staff members would like to believe. While some effort may be made to provide for children in most good hospitals, results are often less than satisfactory.

The nurse may be a keen and reliable source of information about her patients' sleep patterns, food intake, voiding, vomiting and disposition. However, her notes seldom refer to her patients' fears, fantasies or relationships. She seldom has enough time to be available for conversations and play sessions. Staff members may not recognize the value of preparing children for medical experiences and not all feel confident about trying to acquire such knowledge.

Physicians too, may require assistance with young patients,

especially if they do not have pediatric training. Because some children's overwhelming fear prevents them from crying out, doctors are sometimes misled into believing their patient is bearing up well when in fact their patient is seriously upset. Hurt comes in many forms. The mental anguish and emotional trauma of hospitalization may stimulate psychic pain that far outlasts the physical problem.

Play program specialists can assist in offering advice on preparation of children to parents as well as to staff persons. The reduction of anxiety in children prepared for procedures means that the physicians may not need to give sedatives in order to calm down upset children or to use restraints on children because they resist procedures.

Parents may not be successful. Some are more apprehensive than their children and transmit these feelings as though they were contagious. Others over-prepare their children with overwhelming, unnecessary detail unasked for. Still others simply cannot prepare a child because they are themselves unprepared and do not have the information needed.

Toys need to be carefully selected not only for safety and endurance but for emotional and cognitive development as well.

6. "PLAY MAY BE ALL RIGHT WHEN CHILDREN ARE RECUPERATING OR IN THE CLINIC, BUT CHILDREN IN EMERGENCY OR INTENSIVE CARE ARE IN CRITICAL SITUATIONS. WE CAN'T WASTE RESOURCES ON "PLAY."

Particularly in highly critical situations a patient and his family need to be calmed with information, reassurance and consistent attention. At this time the child needs people who understand his fears and answer his questions in a sympathetic and knowledgeable way. Just a few conversations will help and, when the treatment procedures take all of the physician's and nurse's attention, the play director could be available to talk with the child reassuringly. Even unconscious patients, some say, respond to T.L.C. – some knowledgeable physicians talk with unconscious patients as they treat them on the possibility that the patient, if he is hearing anything at all, should hear reassurance.

7. "THIS IS AN ACUTE HOSPITAL. THE CHILDREN ARE HERE ONLY FOR A FEW DAYS. THERE ISN'T TIME ENOUGH FOR THEM TO BE TRAUMATIZED. THEY ARE IN AND OUT BEFORE THEY KNOW IT."

Emotional traumas can be encountered on the first few days of hospitalization because the degree of stress is relative to how a child perceives the event, not to the length of his hospitalization. No adult can judge how much psychological and emotional stress is weighing on a child until the child, drawing upon his own previous experience, his family's attitudes, his beliefs about what is going to happen or has taken place, tells us. When he does, there needs to be a responsible and sympathetic professional ready and willing to help. This need is acute, too.

8. "WE CAN SEE HAVING A PROGRAM IN THE INPATIENT UNIT, BUT WHY IS IT NEEDED IN A CLINIC?"

Children's needs remain constant wherever medical treatment is received. Children view many medical procedures as confusing and threatening, no matter whether they take place in a doctor's office, hospital, or clinic, although hospitalization does add the anxiety of separation from the family and its routines.

In addition, many clinics report an increase of patients whose parents want help with their children's behavioral, school or psychosomatic problems, and observations by trained playroom staff can help physicians in these diagnoses. In the clinic playroom, staff can begin the preparation of children who will require hospitalization and can give continuity to those children with chronic conditions who will have repeated hospitalizations.

9. "ONCE THE PLAY DIRECTOR HAS A PROGRAM GOING WELL ON THE INPATIENT UNIT CAN SHE LEAVE IT IN THE HANDS OF THE VOLUNTEERS, STUDENTS OR NURSES, AND MOVE ON TO START A NEW PROGRAM IN THE CLINIC OR ON ANOTHER FLOOR?"

Yes, a program can "run by itself" without a full-time professional leader if it is well-organized and well-staffed and has enough of the play director's time for support and guidance. However, in that circumstance, the services and the standards of performance will vary according to who is in charge of the program on any particular day. In addition, the quality is certain to deteriorate if there is frequent turnover of volunteers or staff. A certain proportion of situations requiring professional skills and judgment are likely to be missed or mishandled. As in any volunteer program, the road is downhill unless the program is periodically reviewed and jolted with infusions of enthusiasm, discipline and professionalism. It is always preferable to offer a high-level, responsive program in a few areas and to continually remind administrators and others of the need for more staff, services and support in other areas of the facility that deal with children than to spread services or personnel too thin.

10. "IT'S A VERY GOOD IDEA. IF WE HAD THE MONEY, THIS WOULD BE A FINE PROGRAM TO SUPPORT. RIGHT NOW WE CAN'T AFFORD THIS ICING ON THE CAKE."

Some administrators would feel better if there were some revenue collected from the play program. Few hospitals with existing programs do charge an extra fee for their play program. Those that do include a formal school program or are ordinarily reimbursed by the public school or supplied with teachers. There is a profound return from the programs, however. This is most evident in a child's physiological and psychological well-being. Studies have shown significant reductions in vomiting, crying, restless sleep and poor eating in a child whose stress is reduced. The child is seen by the staff as more cooperative and less frightened. Parents report less post-discharge behavior problems. These benefits are not icing to the child or his family.

When a certain amount of money is available and choices must be made, decisions are generally reached by considering priorities. A play program may be competing for funds with other parts of the facility which need technical machinery or additional specialized staff, even when the needs are not easily compared. At this time especially the play program should not be looked upon as of minor significance. It is a good idea, it is indispensible and it is right for children. When deciding whether it deserves maximum support, *the question to ask is whether the hospital can afford not to have it.*

BOOKS TO SUPPLEMENT A STANDARD CHILDREN'S LIBRARY

Bartosh, J. A.: *Kenny Visits the Hospital.* New York, Exposition Press, 1956.

Bennett, Merilyn Brottman and Sanders, Sylvia: *How We Talk.* Minneapolis, Lerner, 1966.

Berger, Terry: *I Have Feelings.* New York, Behavioral Publications, 1971.

Berry, James: *Why You Feel Hot, Why You Feel Cold: Your Body's Temperature.* Boston, Little, Brown, 1973.

Brown, Myra Berry: *Casey's Sore-Throat Day.* New York, Watts, 1964.

Brown, Myra Berry: *First Night Away From Home.* New York, Watts, 1960.

Byrd, Mitzi: *Loneliest Chicken.* New York, Macmillan, 1953.

Chase, Francine: *A Visit to the Hospital.* New York, Grosset and Dunlap, 1958.

Clark, Bettina and Coleman, Lester: *Going to the Hospital.* New York, Random House, 1971.

Cohen, Miriam: *Will I Have a Friend?* New York, Macmillan, 1967.

Collier, J.: *Danny Goes to the Hospital.* New York, Norton, 1970.

Elkin, Benjamin: *Loudest Noise in the World.* New York, Viking, 1954.

Ets, Marie Hall: *Bad Boy, Good Boy.* New York, Crowell, 1967.

Ets, Marie Hall: *Play With Me.* New York, Viking Press, 1955.

Ets, Marie Hall: *Talking Without Words.* New York, Viking, 1968.

Fassler, Joan: *My Grandpa Died Today.* New York, Behavioral Publications, 1971.

Fassler, Joan: *One Little Girl.* New York, Behavioral Publications, 1969.

Fassler, Joan: *The Boy with a Problem.* New York, Behavioral Publications, 1971.

Francoise: *The Things I Like.* New York, Scribner, 1960.

Fryer, Judith: *How We Hear: The Story of Hearing.* Minneapolis, Lerner, 1961.

Garn, Bernard J.: *A Visit to the Dentist.* New York, Grosset and Dunlap, 1959.

Garn, Bernard: *A Visit to the Hospital.* New York, Grosset and Dunlap, 1959.

Gelfand, Ravina and Patterson, Letha: *They Wouldn't Quit.* Minneapolis, Lerner, 1962.

Gilbert, Miriam: *Karen Gets a Fever.* Minneapolis, Lerner, 1961.

Goldin, Augusta: *Straight Hair, Curly Hair.* New York, Crowell, 1966.

Greene, Carla: *I Want to Be a Nurse.* Chicago, Childrens Press, 1957.

Harris, Audrey: *Why Did He Die?* Minneapolis, Lerner, 1965.
Haynes, Olive V.: *The True Book of Health.* Chicago, Childrens Press, 1954.
Health and Growth, Book 1, 2, 3, and teacher's editions. Palo Alto, Scott-Foresman, 1973.
Holman, Felice: *I Hear You Smiling.* New York, Scribner, 1973.
Jones, Raymond F.: *Stories of Great Physicians.* Racine, Whitman, 1963.
Jubelier, Ruth: *About Jack's Dental Checkup.* Illinois, Melmont, 1959.
Jubelier, Ruth: *About Jill's Check-Up.* Illinois, Melmont, 1963.
Krasilovsky, Phyllis: *The Very Little Boy.* Garden City, Doubleday, 1962.
Krishef, Robert K.: *Our Remarkable Feet.* Minneapolis, Lerner, 1968.
Krishef, Robert K.: *Our Wonderful Hands.* Minneapolis, Lerner, 1967.
Lapp, Carolyn: *Dentist's Tools.* Minneapolis, Lerner, 1961.
Lerner, Marguerite: *Dear Little Mumps Child.* Minneapolis, Lerner, 1959.
Lerner, Marguerite: *Doctor's Tools.* Minneapolis, Lerner, 1960.
Lerner, Marguerite: *Michael Gets the Measles.* Minneapolis, Lerner, 1959.
Lerner, Marguerite: *Peter Gets the Chickenpox.* Minneapolis, Lerner, 1959.
LeShan, Eda: *What Makes Me Feel This Way?* New York, Macmillan, 1972.
Livaudais, Madileine and Dunne, Robert: *The Skeleton Book.* New York, Walker, 1972.
Marks, Geoffrey: *Women in White.* New York, Scribner, 1972.
McGovern, Ann: *The Question and Answer Book About the Human Body.* New York, Random House, 1965.
McNamara, Louise G. and Litchfield, Ada B.: *Your Busy Brain.* Boston, Little, Brown, 1973.
McNamara, Louise G. and Litchfield, Ada B.: *Your Growing Cells.* Boston, Little, Brown, 1973.
McNamara, Louise G. and Litchfield, Ada B.: *Your Living Bones.* Boston, Little, Brown, 1973.
Milgrom, Harry: *ABC Science Experiments.* New York, Collier Books, 1973.
Olshaker, B.: *Tommy's Tonsillectomy.* Washington, Marco Books, 1958.
Rowland, Florence: *Let's Go to a Hospital.* New York, Putnam, 1968.
Sands, George J.: *Why Glasses: the Story of Vision.* Minneapolis, Lerner, 1960.
Scarry, Patricia M.: *Let's Visit the Dentist.* Racine, Golden, 1970.
Schick, Eleanor: *Making Friends.* New York, Macmillan, 1969.
Schloat, G. Warren: *Your Wonderful Teeth.* New York, Scribner, 1954.
Schneider, Herman and Schneider, Nina: *How Your Body Works.* New York, Scott, 1949.
Sendal, Maurice: *Where the Wild Things Are.* New York, Harper and Row, 1963.
Sever, Josephine A.: *Johnny Goes to the Hospital.* New York, Houghton Mifflin, 1953.
Shay, Arthur: *What Happens When You Go to the Hospital.* Chicago, Reilly and Lee, 1969.

Showers, Paul: *Drop of Blood.* New York, Crowell, 1967.
Vermeer, Jackie and Lariviere, Marian: *The Little Kid's Craft Book.* New York, Taplinger, 1973.
Vinson, Pauline: *Willie Goes to the Hospital.* New York, Macmillan, 1956.
Weber, A.: *Elizabeth Get Well.* New York, Crowell, 1970.
Wittels, Harriet and Greisman, Joan: *Things I Hate.* New York, Behavioral Publications, 1971.
Zim, Herbert: *What's Inside of Me?* New York, Morrow, 1952.

BIBLIOGRAPHY

A Useful List of Classroom Items That Can Be Scrounged or Purchased. Early Childhood Education Study, EDC, 55 Chapel St., Newton, Mass. 02160

Aisenberg, Ruth B.; Wolff, Peter H.; Rosenthal, Amnon; and Nadas, Alexander S.: Psychological impact of cardiac catheterization. *Pediatrics, 51*:105, 1973.

Alison's tonsillectomy is a family operation. *Today's Health, 51*:50, 1973.

Allen, Eileen; Dmitriev, Valentine; and Hayden, Alice: Early warning: observation as a tool for recognizing potential handicaps in young children. *Educational Horizons, 50*:43, Winter 1971-72.

Almy, Millie: *Ways of Studying Children.* New York, Teachers College, Columbia University, 1972.

Altschuler, Anne: Children's books about hospitalization. *ACCH Newsletter, 1*:7, 1973.

Amen, Elisabeth W. and Renison, Nancy: A study of the relationship between play patterns and anxiety in young children. *Genet Psychol Monogr, 50*:3, 1954.

Andrew, June M.: Recovery from surgery with and without preparatory instruction for three coping styles. *J Pers Soc Psychol, 15*:223, 1970.

Arneson, S. A.: Changes in a toddler's mode of adapting to separation from his mother during daily relationship experiences with one nurse. *ANA Clin Sess* :134, 1968.

Aufhauser, T.: Child in the hospital. *AORN Journal, 13*:75, 1971.

Axline, Virginia: *Dibs.* New York, Ballantine, 1969.

Ayrault, Evelyn West: *Helping the Handicapped Teenager Mature.* New York, Association Press, 1971.

Azarnoff, Pat: A play program in a pediatric clinic. *Children, 17*:218, 1970.

Azarnoff, Pat: Volunteers assist in child activities. *Hospitals, JAHA, 46*:61, 1972.

Azarnoff, Pat: Volunteer-supervised play teaches and comforts young patients. *The Volunteer Leader, 8*:10, 1972.

Barnes, Corinne M.; Kenny, Frederic M.; Call, Thomas; and Reinhart, John B.: Measurement in management of anxiety in children for open heart surgery. *Pediatrics, 49*:250, 1972.

Barsch, Ray H.: *The Parent of the Handicapped Child.* Springfield, Thomas, 1968.

Barten, Harvey H. (Ed.): *Brief Therapies.* New York, Behavioral Publications, 1971.

Barton, Pauline H.: Play as a tool of nursing. *Nurs Outlook, 10*:162, 1962.

Beers, N.: Helping the preschool blind child in the hospital. *Hospitals, JAHA, 32*:32, 1958.

Beker, Jerome; Husted, Shirle M.; Gitelson, Paul M.; Kaminstein, Philip; and Adler, Lois Finkel: *Critical Incidents in Child Care*. New York, Behavioral Publications, 1972.

Bell, A.: Psychological preparation of child contributes to success of surgery. *Hosp Top, 49*:78, 1971.

Berger, Allan S.: Anxiety in young children. *Young Children, 27*:5, 1971.

Bernstein, Dorothy M.: After transplantation — the child's emotional reactions. In Chess, Stella, and Thomas, A. (Eds.): *Annual Progress in Child Psychiatry and Child Development*. New York, Brunner/Mazel, 1972.

Bielicka, Izabela and Olechnowicz, Hanna: Treating children traumatized by hospitalization. *Child, 10*:194, 1963.

Blake, Florence G.: *Open Heart Surgery in Children*. Public Health Service Publication No. 2075, 1970.

Blumgart, Eleanor and Korsch, Barbara M.: Pediatric recreation; an approach to meeting the needs of hospitalized children. *Pediatrics, 34*:133, 1964.

Bopp, Jane (Ed.): *Guidelines for the development of hospital programs for the personnel conducting programs of therapeutic play for pediatric patients*. Union, W.V., Association for Care of Children in Hospitals, P.O. Box 11, 24983

Boston Children's Medical Center, members of the staff and Gregg, Elizabeth M.: *What to Do When "There's Nothing to Do."* New York, Dell, 1968.

Bowlby, John: *Attachment and Loss: Attachment*. Vol. I. New York, Basic Books, 1969.

Bowlby, John: *Attachment and Loss: Separation*. Vol. II. London, Hogarth Press, 1973.

Branstetter, E.: The young child's response to hospitalization: separation anxiety or lack of mothering care? *AJPH, 59*:92, 1969.

Brazelton, T. Berry: *Infants and Mothers*. New York, Delacorte Press, 1969.

Brazelton, T. Berry: Multidisciplined patient care rounds. *Pediatrics, 43*: 469, 1969.

Brazelton, T. Berry; Holder, Richmond; and Talbot, Beatrice: Emotional aspects of rheumatic fever in children. *J Pediatr, 43*:339, 1953.

Brim, Orville G., Jr.; Freeman, Howard E.; Levine, Sol; and Scotch, Norman A.: *The Dying Patient*. New York, Russell Sage Foundation, 1970.

Brinkhous, Kenneth M.: Changing prospects of children with hemophilia. *Children, 17*:222, 1970.

Brooks, Mary: Why play in the hospital? *Nurs Clin North Am, 5*:431, 1970.

Brown, Margaret J.: Preadmission orientation for children and parents. *Can Nurs, 67*:29, 1971.

Buist, Charlotte A. and Schulman, Jerome L.: *Toys and Games for Educationally Handicapped Children*. Springfield, Thomas, 1969.

Byler, Ruth; Lewis, Gertrude; and Totman, Ruth: *Teach Us What We Want to Know*. New York, Mental Health Materials Center, 1969.

Cain, Albert C.; Fast, Irene; and Erickson, Mary: Children's disturbed reactions to the death of a sibling. *Am J Orthopsychiatry, 34*:741, 1964.

Carbonara, Nancy T.: *Techniques for Observing Normal Child Behavior*. Pittsburgh, University of Pittsburg Press, 1969.

Care of Children in Hospitals. Evanston, American Academy of Pediatrics, 1970.

Carmichael, Viola S.: *Science Experiences for Young Children*. Southern California Association for the Education of Young Children, P.O. Box 691, Sierra Madre, California, 91024

Carrier, Rick: *Action! Camera! Super 8 Cassette Film Making for Beginners*. New York, Scribner, 1972.

Carson, R.: When a child goes to the hospital. *Family Circle, 68*:50, 1966.

Doward, Barbara: *Teaching Aids and Toys for Handicapped Children*. Washington, D.C., The Council for Exceptional Children, 1201 16th St., 1960.

Duran, Maria T.: Family-centered care and the adolescent's quest for self-identity. *Nurs Clin North Am, 7*:65, 1972.

Eichenbaum, I. and Dunn, N.: Projective drawings by children under repeated dental stress. *J Dent Child, 38*:164, 1971.

Englebardt, S. L.: Care-by-parent relieves emotional strain on children, financial strain on parents. *Mod Hosp, 113*:94, 1969.

Engleman, J. L.; Engleman, E.; and Fink, D.: Playroom in the outpatient clinic; everyone benefits. *Hospitals, JAHA, 44*:47, 1970.

Equipment and Supplies. Washington, D.C., Association for Childhood Education, Int., 3615 Wisconsin Ave., N.W., 20016.

Erickson, Florence: Play interviews for four-year-old hospitalized children. *Monogr Soc Res Child Dev*, 3, 1958.

Evans, A. and Edin, S.: If a Child Must Die. *N Engl J Med, 278*:138, 1968.

Falstein, E. I.; Judas, I.; and Mendelsohn, R. S.: Fantasies in children prior to herniorrhaphy. *Am J Orthopsychiatry, 27*:800, 1957.

Field, William E.: Watch your message. *Am J Nurs, 72*:1278, 1972.

Finnie, Nancie R.: *Handling the Young Cerebral Palsied Child at Home*. New York, Dutton, 1970.

Flandorf, V. S.: *Books to Help Children Adjust to a Hospital*, Chicago, American Library Association, 1967.

Freiberg, K.: How parents react when their child is hospitalized. *Am J Nurs, 72*:1270, 1972.

Fretz, Bruce R.; Johnson, Warren R.; and Johnson, Julia A.: Intellectual and perceptual motor development as a function of therapeutic play. *Res Q Am Assoc Health Phys Educ, 40*:687, 1969.

Freud, Anna: Role of bodily illness in the mental life of children. *Psychoanal Study Child,* 7:69, 1952.

Freud, Anna: *The Psychoanalytical Treatment of Children.* New York, Schocken, 1964.

Gallagher, J. Roswell: Rest and restriction: their conflict with an adolescent's development. *Am J. Public Health,* 46:1424, 1956.

Geis, R.: Home visits help prepare preschoolers and their parents for hospitalization. *ANA Regional Clinical Conferences,* 1967.

Gellert, Elizabeth; Girgus, Joan S.; and Cohen, Jacob: Children's awareness of their bodily appearance: a developmental study of factors associated with the body percept. *Genet Psychol Monogr,* 84:109, 1971.

Gellert, Elizabeth: Reducing the emotional stresses of hospitalization for children. *Am J Occup Ther,* 12:125, 1958.

Gibbs, N.: Problems of play and mastery in the blind child. *Dev Med Child Neurol,* 11:516, 1969.

Glaser, Helen H. (Ed.): *Ideas and Activities with Hospitalized Children.* Union, W.Va., Association for Care of Children in Hospitals, P.O. Box H, 24983, 1970.

Glidewell, John: Parental attitudes and child behavior. In *Conference on Community Mental Health Research.* Springfield, Thomas, 1961.

Gordon, Ira J.: *Baby Learning Through Baby Play.* New York, St. Martin's Press, 1970.

Green, M. and Segar, W. E.: A new design for patient care and pediatric education in a children's hospital: an interview report. *Pediatrics,* 28: 825, 1961.

Grollman, Earl A.: *Explaining Death to Children.* Boston, Beacon, 1967.

Grossman, Frances K.: *Brothers and Sisters of Retarded Children: An Exploratory Study.* Syracuse, Syracuse University Press, 1972.

Hall, Edward T.: *The Silent Language.* Garden City, New York, Doubleday, 1959.

Hall, Elvajean: *Personal Problems of Children.* Boston, Campbell and Hall, 1964.

Hardgrove, Carol B. and Dawson, Rosemary B.: *Parents and Children in the Hospital.* Boston, Little, Brown, 1972.

Hartley, Ruth E.; Frank, Lawrence K.; and Goldenson, Robert M.: *Understanding Children's Play.* New York, Columbia, 1952.

Heffernan, Michael and Azarnoff, Pat: Factors in reducing children's anxiety about clinic visits. *HSMHA Health Reports,* 86:1131, 1971.

Hoffman, Irwin and Futterman, Edward H.: Coping with waiting: psychiatric intervention and study in the waiting room of a pediatric oncology clinic. *Compr Psychiatry,* 12:67, 1971.

Hofman, Adele D. and Gaman, Milton: The adolescent outpatient. *Postgrad Med,* 51:245, 1971.

Homan, William E.: *Child Sense.* New York, Bantam, 1970.

Home visits prepare children for surgery. *JAMA, 219*:680, 1972.

Hunnisett, Frank and Knowles, David: Orienting prospective patients. *Hospitals, JAHA, 44*:51, 1970.

Hurry A. and Sandler, J.: Coping with reality: the child's defences against the external world. *Br J Med Psychol, 44*:379, 1971.

Issner, N.: The family of the hospitalized child. *Nurs Clin North Am, 7*:5, 1972.

Jackson, K.; Winkley, R.; Faust, O. A.; Cermak, E. G.; and Burtt, M. M.: Behavior changes indicating emotional trauma in tonsillectomized children. *Pediatrics, 12*:23, 1953.

Johnson, Dorothy E.: Powerlessness: a significant determinant in patient behavior. *J Nurs Educ, 6*:39, 1967.

Jolly, Hugh: Play and the sick child. *Lancet, 2*:1286, 1968.

Kangery, Rosemarie: Children's answers: how it feels to be in hospital was described by fifty children in a recent study. *Am J Nurs, 60*:1748, 1960.

Karon, Myron and Vernick, Joel: An approach to the emotional support of fatally ill child. *Clin Pediatr, 7*:274, 1968.

Kassowitz, K.: Psychodynamic reactions of children to the use of hypodermic needles. *A.M.A. Journal of Diseases of Children*, 95:253, 1958.

Kastenbaum, Robert and Aisenberg, Ruth: *The Psychology of Death.* New York, Springer, 1972.

Kessler, Jane: *Psychopathology of Children.* Engelwood Cliffs, Prentice-Hall, 1966.

Kjer, Dell C., (chairman): The Significance of the Young Child's Motor Development. Proceedings of a conference. Washington D.C., National Association for the Education of Young Children, 1971.

Kliman, Gilbert: *Psychological Emergencies of Childhood.* New York, Grune and Stratton, 1968.

Korsch, Barbara; Gozzi, Ethel K.; and Francis, Vida: Gaps in doctor-patient communication. *Pediatrics, 42*:855, 1968.

Kunzman, Lucy: Some factors influencing a young child's mastery of hospitalization. *Nurs Clin North Am, 1*:13, 1972.

Lally, Ronald J.; Honig, Alice S.; and Caldwell, Bettye M.: Training paraprofessionals for work with infants and toddlers. *Young Children, 28*: 173, 1973.

Landsman, Eleanor: The function of a play program in pediatrics. *Pediatric Annals, 1*:64, 1972.

Levinson, Boris M.: *Pet-Oriented Child Psychotherapy.* Springfield, Thomas, 1969.

Linde, Leonard; Rasof, Beatrice; Dunn, Olive J.; and Rabb, Ethel: Attitudinal factors in congenital heart disease. *Pediatrics, 38*:92, 1966.

Linden, J. I. and Stollak, G. E.: The training of undergraduates in play techniques. *J Clin Psychol, 25*:213, 1969.

Loomis, W. G.: Management of children's emotional reactions to severe body damage (burns). *Clin Pediatr,* 9:362, 1970.

Love, Harold; Henderson, Shirley; and Stewart, Mary: *Your Child Goes to the Hospital.* Springfield, Thomas, 1972.

Lovell, K.; Hoyle, H. W.; and Siddall, M. Q.: A study of some aspects of the play and language of young children with delayed speech. *J Child Psychol Psychiatry,* 9:41, 1968.

Marion, Marian C.: Create a parent-space – a place to stop, look, and read. *Young Children, 28*:221, 1973.

Mason, Edward A.: The hospitalized child – his emotional needs. *N Engl J Med, 272*:406, 1965.

Matheny, A. P. Jr. and Vernick, J.: Parents of the mentally retarded child: emotionally overwhelmed or informationally deprived? *J Pediatr, 74*:953, 1969.

Matterson, E. M.: *Play and Playthings for the Preschool Child.* Baltimore, Penguin, 1967.

Mattson, Ake and Weisberg, Israel: Behavioral reactions to minor illness in preschool children. *Pediatrics, 46*:604, 1970.

May, J. G.: A psychiatric study of a pediatric intensive therapy unit. A child psychiatrist looks at the emotional responses of children and staff in this treatment setting. *Clin Pediatr, 11*:76, 1972.

Maynard, Marjorie and Dondero, Anne: Nurses gain from field work with young children. *Young Children, 24*:298, 1969.

McCaffery, Margo: Children's responses to rectal temperatures. *Nurs Res, 20*:32, 1971.

McDonald, Eugene: *Understand Those Feelings.* Pennsylvania, Stanwix, 1962.

Mechanic, D.: The influence of mothers on their children's health attitudes and behavior. *Pediatrics, 53*:444, 1964.

Michal-Smith, Harold: *The Exceptional Child in the Normal Nursery.* New York, Early Childhood Education Council, 32-16 166th St., Flushing, 11358, 1970.

Millar, Susanna: *The Psychology of Play.* Baltimore, Penguin Books, 1968.

Millar, T. P.: The hospital and the preschool child. *Children, 17*:171, 1970.

Missildine, Hugh W.: *Your Inner Child of the Past.* New York, Simon and Schuster, 1963.

Moor, Pauline M.: *A Blind Child, Too, Can Go to Nursery School.* New York, American Foundation for the Blind, 15 W 16th St., 1952.

Morgenstern, F. S.: Psychological handicaps in the play of handicapped children. *Dev Med Child Neurol, 10*:115, 1968.

Morse, Joan: The goal of life enhancement for a fatally ill child. *Children, 17*:63, 1970.

Moustakas, Clark E.: *Psychotherapy with Children.* New York, Ballantine, 1970.

Mycue, Elena De Los Santos: *Young Children with Handicaps; Part IV,*

Resources: Directories, Newsletters, Bibliographies and General Information. Urbana, ERIC Clearinghouse on Early Childhood Education, University of Illinois at Urbana-Champaign, 805 W. Pennsylvania Ave, 61801.

Needs of Children in the Hospital. Union, W.Va., Association for Care of Children, P.O. Box H, 24983, 1971.

Nelson, Alice C.: How can you stand the crying? *Am J Nurs, 70*:66, 1970.

Northcott, Winifred N.: The integration of young deaf children into ordinary educational programs. *Except Child, 38*:29, 1971.

Parmelee, Arthur Jr.: A pediatrician's plan for mental hygiene. *Ment Hyg, 38*:261, 1954.

Parmelee, A. H. Jr. and Liverman, L.: Blindness in infants and children. In Green, M. and Haggerty, R. J. (Eds.): *Ambulatory Pediatrics.* New York, Saunders, 1968.

Parmelee, A. H. Jr. and Liverman, L.: The elementary school in medical education. *J Med Educ, 9*:655, 1958.

Parsonage, S.: Preparation of children going into hospital. *Dist Nurs, 14*:30, 1971.

Pedersen, F. A. and Robson, K. S.: Father participation in infancy. *Am J* Orthopsychiatry, 39:466, 1969.

Peterson, D. R.: Behavior problems of middle childhood. *J Cons Psychol, 25*:205, 1961.

Petrillo, Madeline and Sanger, Sirgay: *Emotional Care of Hospitalized Children.* Philadelphia, Lippincott, 1972.

Petrillo, Madeline: Preparing children and parents for hospital and treatment. *Pediatric Annals, 1*:24, 1972.

Pickett, L. K.: The hospital environment for the pediatric surgical patient. *Pediatr Clin North Am, 16*:531, 1969.

Pierce, William D.; Tricket, Edison J.; and Moss, Rudolf, H.: Changing ward atmosphere through staff discussion of the perceived ward environment. *Arch Gen Psychiatric, 26*:35, 1972.

Plank, E.: *Working with Children in Hospitals.* Chicago, Case Western Reserve University Press, 1971.

Pounds, Valerie A.: Play therapy. *Nurs Times, 65*:769, 1969.

Prugh, Dane G.: Investigations dealing with the reactions of children and families to hospitalization and illness: problems and potentialities. In Caplan, Gerald (Ed.): *Emotional Problems of Early Childhood.* New York, Basic, 1955.

Quinby, S.: How children live after disfiguring burns. *Psychiatry Med, 2*: 146, 1971.

Redl, Fritz: Strategy and techniques of the life space interview. *Am J Orthopsychiatry, 29*:1, 1959.

Rees, Elizabeth Lodge: *A Doctor Looks at Toys.* Springfield, Thomas, 1961.

Rich, John: *Interviewing Children and Adolescents.* New York, Macmillan, 1968.

Rie, Herbert E.; Boverman, Harold; Grossman, Burton J.; and Ozoa, Natividad: Immediate and long-term effects of interventions early in prolonged hospitalization. *Pediatrics, 41*:755, 1968.

Rieger, Edythe: *Science Adventures in Children's Play.* New York, Play Schools Association, 1968.

Riese, Hertha: *Heal the Hurt Child.* Chicago, University of Chicago Press, 1962.

Rigg, C. A. and Fisher, Rona C.: Is a separate adolescent ward worthwhile? *Am J Dis Child, 122*:489, 1971.

Ritchie, M. A.: The hospital schoolroom. *Am J Nurs, 63*:77, 1963.

Robertson, James: *Hospitals and Children: A Parent's Eye View.* New York, International Universities Press, 1964.

Robinson, David: Mother's fears, their children's well being in hospital, and the study of illness behavior. *Br J Prev Soc Med, 22*:228, 1968.

Roseke, Nancy A.: The junior medical student as diagnostician of the family of an emotionally disturbed child. *J Med Educ, 47*:51, 1972.

Rosenthal, A. J. and Levine, S. V.: Brief psychotherapy with children: process of therapy. In Rosenthal, A. J. and Levine, S. V.: *Annual Progress in Child Psychiatry and Child Development.* New York, Bruner/Mazel, 1972.

Rosenthal, M. K.: The generalization of dependency behavior from mother to stranger. *J Child Psychol Psychiatry, 8*:117, 1967.

Rothenberg, M.: Child psychiatry – pediatrics liaison: a history and commentary. *J Am Acad Child Psychiatry, 7*:492, 1968.

Rothenberg, Robert E.: *Understanding Surgery.* New York, Pocket Books, 1965.

Routh, Thomas A.: *The Volunteer and Community Agencies.* Springfield, Thomas, 1972.

Roy, Mary C.: Role cues and mothers of hospitalized children. *Nurs Res, 16*:178, 1967.

Sabot, Lawrence M.; Peck, Rosalind; and Raskin, Jack: The waiting room society. *Arch Gen Psychiatry, 21*:25, 1969.

Sadler, John E. Jr.: Coordinated pediatric care through a liaison team. *Pediatric Annals, 1*:72, 1972.

Salk, Lee: *What Every Child Would Like His Parents to Know.* New York, McKay, 1972.

Sauer, J.: Preadmission orientation: effect on patient manageability. *Hosp Top, 46*:79, 1968.

Scahill, Mary: Preparing children for procedures and operations. *Nurs Outlook, 17*:36, 1969.

Schaffer, H. R. and Callender, W. W.: Psychologic effects of hospitalization in infancy. *Pediatrics, 24*:528, 1959.

Schowalter, John E.: The utilization of child psychiatry on a pediatric adolescent ward. *J Am Acad Child Psychiatry, 10*:1684; 1971.

Schowalter, John E. and Lord, Ruth D.: The hospitalized adolescent. *Children, 18*:127, 1971.

Schowalter, John E. and Solnit, A.: Child psychology consultation in a general hospital emergency room. *J Am Acad Child Psychiatry, 5*:534, 1966.

Schultz, Nancy V.: How children perceive pain. *Nurs Outlook, 19*:670, 1971.

Schwartz, A. H.: Children's concepts of research hospitalization. *N Engl J Med, 287*:589, 1972.

Schwartz, Alvin: *The Rainy Day Book.* New York, Trident Press, 1968.

Seidelman, James E. and Mintonyo, Grace: *Shopping Cart Art.* New York, Macmillan, 1970.

Shaw, Jane: Volunteers prepare children for surgery through puppet therapy. *Mod Hosp, 14*:126, 1970.

Shoemaker, Rowena M.: *All in Play.* New York, Play Schools Association.

Shore, Milton J. (Ed.): *Red is the color of hurting.* U.S. Dept. of HEW, #1583, 1967.

Shore, Milton; Geiser, Robert L.; and Wolman, Harold M.: Constructive uses of a hospital experience. *Children, 12*:3, 1965.

Smith, A. M.: *Play for Convalescent Children in Hospitals and at Home.* New York, Barnes, 1961.

Smith, R. M.: Preparing children for anesthesia and surgery. *Am J Dis Child, 101*:650, 1961.

Smith, W. G.: Critical life-events and prevention strategies in mental health. *Arch Gen Psychiatry, 25*:103, 1971.

Solky, C. G. and Hoekelman, R. A.: The pediatric emergency department: locus for recognition of psychosocial disability. *Clin Pediatr, 10*:524, 1971.

Solnit, A. J.: Hospitalization: aid to physical and psychological health in childhood. *J Dis Child, 99*:155, 1960.

Solomons, G. and Solomons, H. C.: The physician and psychological appraisal. *Dev Med Child Neurol, 15*:95, 1973.

Some current therapeutic use of animals in a hospital setting. *Recreation, 54*:415, 1961.

Stein, A.: Observations on socioprofessional factors mitigating against the psychological care of hospitalized children. *Ment Hyg, 48*:424, 1964.

Stein, A.: Resistance to psychological prophylaxis in hospital pediatrics. *J Pediatr, 55*:497, 1959.

Stein, Stefan and Charles, Edward: Emotional factors in juvenile diabetes mellitus: a study of early life experience of adolescent diabetics. *Am J Psychiatry, 128*:700, 1971.

Stevenson, Harold W. and Stevenson, Nancy G.: A method for simultaneous observation and analysis of children's behavior. *J Genet Psychol, 99*:253, 1961.

Stocking, Myron; Rothney, W.; Grosser, G.; and Goodwin, R.: Psychopathology in the pediatric hospital: implications for the pediatrician. *Psychiatry Med, 1*:329, 1970.

The hospitalized child, his family, and his community. Union, W.Va., Association for Care of Children in Hospitals, P.O. Box H, 24983, 1970.

Tisza, Veronica B.; Hurwitz, Irving; and Angoff, Kristine: The use of a play program by hospitalized children. *J Am Acad Child Psychiatry, 9*:515, 1970.

Troutman, K. C. and Mayer, B. W.: Suggestions for parents of children who are to be admitted for dental oral rehabilitation. *J Am Dent Assoc, 82*: 388, 1971.

Vance, V. J. and Taylor, W. F.: Psychosocial problems in a pediatric allergy clinic. *Ann Allergy, 29*:582, 1971.

Vernick, Joel: The use of the life space interview on a medical ward. *Social Casework, 44*:465, 1963.

Vernick, Joel and Lunceford, Janet L.: Milieu design for adolescents with leukemia. *Am J Nurs, 67*:559, 1967.

Vernon, David T. A.; Foley, Jeanne M.; Sipowicz, Raymond R.; and Schulman, Jerome L.: *The Psychological Responses of Children to Hospitalization and Illness.* Springfield, Thomas, 1965.

Vredevoe, Donna L.; Kim, Audrey C.; Dambacher, Betty M.; and Call, Justin, D.: Aggressive post-operative play responses of hospitalized preschool children. *Nursing Research Report, 4*:1, 1969.

Webb, M.: Tactics to reduce a child's fear of pain. *Am J Nurs, 66*:2699; 1966.

Wheeler, W. E.: Recollections of 40 years of hospitalization of children. *Pediatr Res, 6*:840, 1972.

White, Patrick: Hospital recreation helps adolescent patients. *Can Nurs, 68*:34, 1972.

Whitson, Betty J.: The puppet treatment in pediatrics. *Am J Nurs, 72*:1612, 1972.

Whitted, B. A. and Scott, R. B.: The significance of a play program in the care of children in a general hospital. *J Natl Med Assoc, 54*:488, 1962.

Wilson, Madeline (Ed.): *Obstacles to Optimal Care.* Union, W.Va., Association for Care of Children in Hospitals, P.O. Box H, 24983, 1973.

Winnicott, D. W.: Playing: its theoretical status in the clinical situation. *Int J Psychoanal, 49*:591, 1968.

Wolf, Richard: The hospital and the child. In Solnit, Albert, and Provence, Sally (Eds.): *Modern Perspectives in Child Development.* New York, International Universities Press, 1963.

Wolff, S.: *Children Under Stress.* London, Penguin Press, 1969.

Wright, Beatrice A.: *Physical Disability: A Psychological Approach.* New York, Harper & Row, 1960.

Wu, R.: Explaining treatments to young children. *Am J Nurs, 7*:71, 1965.

INDEX